THE 365 MOST IMPORTANT EVENTS
OF THE TWENTIETH CENTURY

THE

365 MOST

IMPORTANT EVENTS

OF THE

TWENTIETH

CENTURY

Paul Baldwin

—

WILLIAM MORROW AND COMPANY, INC.

NEW YORK

Library of Congress Cataloging-in-Publication Data
Baldwin, Paul.
    The 365 most important events of the twentieth century / Paul
Baldwin. — 1st ed.
        p.   cm.
    ISBN 0-688-15628-2
    1. History, Modern—20th century—Chronology.   2. Twentieth
century—Miscellanea.   I. Title.   II. Title: Three hundred sixty-
five most important events of the twentieth century.
D421.B25   1999
909.82'02'02 — dc21   99–18702
                        CIP

Printed in the United States of America

First Edition

1   2   3   4   5   6   7   8   9   10

BOOK DESIGN BY RICHARD ORIOLO

www.williammorrow.com

TO ESTHER RUTH DAVIS

SECOND MOTHER AND FRIEND
FOR HALF A CENTURY

ACKNOWLEDGMENTS

More than two hundred sources in numerous fields were consulted during the writing of this book, but several "timeline" books were particularly helpful in establishing events to be covered, including *The Timetables of History* by Bernard Grun and Daniel Jo Boorstin (Simon & Schuster, 1979) and *Chronology of the 20th Century* by Philip Waller and John Rowett (Helicon Publishing Ltd., 1995). More specialized sources that proved especially useful were the series of books on World War II (Time-Life Books, 1981), *The People's Almanac* by David Wallechinsky and Irving Wallace (Doubleday and Company, 1975), *Predicting the Future: From Jules Verne to Bill Gates* by John Malone (M. Evans and Company, 1997), and *The Glory and the Dream* by William Manchester (Bantam Doubleday Dell, 1990).

CONTENTS

INTRODUCTION

1. 1900—First Picasso Exhibition in Paris   3

2. 1900—William McKinley Reelected   3

3. 1900—Cameras for Everyone   4

4. 1900—Hawaii and Puerto Rico Become U.S. Territories   4

5. 1900—Discovery of the Minoans   5

6. 1900—Publication of *The Wonderful Wizard of Oz*   5

7. 1900—Art Nouveau Subways   6

8. 1901—Death of Queen Victoria   7

9. 1901—The Nobel Prizes   7

10. 1901—The Assembly Line   8

11. 1901—"Pomp and Circumstance"   8

12. 1902—Ballot Initiatives   9

13. 1902—Caruso's First Recording   9

14. 1902—Hormones Discovered   10

15. 1902—*Just So Stories*   10

16. 1902—The Rose Bowl   11

17. 1902—*The Three Sisters*   11

18. 1903—The Flying Machine   13

19. 1903—First Primary Elections   13

20. 1903—A Message Sent Around the World   14

21. 1903—The World Series   14

22. 1903—The Tour de France   15

23. 1903—The Harley-Davidson Motorcycle 15

24. 1904—Helen Keller Graduates from Radcliffe College 17

25. 1904—Yellow Fever Control 17

26. 1904—The Tea Bag 18

27. 1904—Safety Razor Blades 18

28. 1904—First American Subway 19

29. 1904—*The Great Train Robbery* 19

30. 1904—Theodore Roosevelt Wins Landslide Victory 20

31. 1904—The St. Louis Exposition 20

32. 1904—*Madama Butterfly* 21

33. 1904—*Peter Pan* 21

34. 1905—U.S. Army Submarines 23

35. 1905—Novocaine 23

36. 1905—*The Merry Widow* 24

37. 1905—The Audubon Society 24

38. 1906—A New Formula for Coca-Cola 26

39. 1906—The Forward Pass 26

40. 1906—San Francisco Earthquake 26

41. 1907—The Electric Washing Machine 28

42. 1907—Conservation 28

43. 1907—Daily Comic Strip 29

44. 1907—Corporate Campaign Contributions Outlawed 29

45. 1908—The Model-T 30

46. 1908—William H. Taft Is Elected 30

47. 1909—Freud Visits America 31

48. 1910—Marie Curie Isolates Radium 32

49. 1910—The Boy Scouts   32

50. 1910—The Return of Halley's Comet   33

51. 1910—Equal Billing for Black Performer   34

52. 1910—Mount Wilson Telescope   34

53. 1911—Adoption of Greenwich Mean Time   36

54. 1911—Amundsen Reaches the South Pole   36

55. 1911—Rupert Brooke's *Poems*   37

56. 1911—Traffic Control   37

57. 1911—Standard Oil Is Broken Up   38

58. 1911—*Der Rosenkavalier*   38

59. 1912—The SOS Distress Code   40

60. 1912—Parachuting   40

61. 1912—The Concept of Continental Drift   41

62. 1912—The Consumer Price Index   41

63. 1912—Woodrow Wilson Elected President   42

64. 1912—Piltdown Man, the ''Missing Link''   42

65. 1912—Massachusetts Sets Minimum Wage   43

66. 1912—Hollywood Studios   44

67. 1912—The Keystone Comedies   44

68. 1913—Income Taxes   46

69. 1913—B'nai B'rith Anti-Defamation League   46

70. 1913—The *Rite of Spring*   47

71. 1913—Irish Home Rule Defeated   47

72. 1914—Shakespeare at the Old Vic   49

73. 1914—Assassination of Archduke Franz Ferdinand   49

74. 1914—The ''St. Louis Blues''   50

75. 1914—The Elastic Brassiere   50

76. 1914—The Machine Gun   51

77. 1914—Battle of the Marne   51

78. 1915—Transcontinental Phone Service   53

79. 1915—"The Metamorphosis"   53

80. 1916—First Birth Control Clinic   54

81. 1916—First Woman Elected to U.S. Congress   54

82. 1916—Einstein's General Theory of Relativity   55

83. 1916—Wilson Narrowly Wins Reelection   55

84. 1916—The Battle of the Somme   56

85. 1916—Louis Brandeis Named to the Supreme
     Court   57

86. 1916—Clarence Birdseye's Frozen Food
     Experiments   57

87. 1917—United States Enters World War I   58

88. 1917—The Draft   58

89. 1917—The Russian Revolution   59

90. 1917—*Pravda*   60

91. 1917—The Word "Surrealist" Is Coined   60

92. 1917—Technicolor Movies   61

93. 1917—"Ready-mades" as Art   62

94. 1917—The Pulitzer Prizes   62

95. 1918—Spanish Flu Epidemic   64

96. 1918—Daylight Saving Time   65

97. 1918—Knute Rockne Becomes Coach at Notre
     Dame   65

98. 1919—The Treaty of Versailles   67

99. 1919—Prohibition Ratified   67

100. 1919—First Nonstop Flight Across Atlantic   68

101. 1920—Commercial Radio   70

102. 1920—The Plague in India   70

103. 1920—Robots   71

104. 1920—Hercule Poirot Makes His Entrance   71

105. 1920—Women Get the Vote   72

106. 1920—Miss America   73

107. 1920—Warren G. Harding Elected President   74

108. 1920—League of Women Voters   74

109. 1920—100 Million Strong   75

110. 1921—Ku Klux Klan Resurfaces   76

111. 1921—Germany Given $132 Billion Reparations
     Bill   76

112. 1921—Tomb of the Unknown Soldier   77

113. 1921—The Perfume of the Century   78

114. 1922—*Reader's Digest*   79

115. 1922—*Abie's Irish Rose*   79

116. 1922—*The Waste Land*   80

117. 1923—Tut-Ankh-Amen's Inner Tomb Opened   81

118. 1923—Earthquake in Japan Kills 500,000   81

119. 1923—Sound Pictures   82

120. 1923—The Charleston   82

121. 1924—The First Winter Olympics   84

122. 1924—J. Edgar Hoover   84

123. 1924—Weissmuller Sets World Record   85

124. 1924—Calvin Coolidge Elected in His Own Right   86

125. 1924—Native Americans Given Citizenship   86

126. 1924—*Billy Budd*   87

127. 1925—Scotch Tape Invented   89

CONTENTS

128. 1925—The "Monkey Trial"   89

129. 1925—*The New Yorker* Founded   90

130. 1925—George Bernard Shaw Wins the Nobel Prize   91

131. 1925—Country Music Gains Popularity   92

132. 1926—The Eight-Hour Day   93

133. 1926—Gertrude Ederle Swims the English Channel   93

134. 1926—Book-of-the-Month Club Founded   94

135. 1926—The Death of Valentino   94

136. 1926—Liquid Fuel Rocket   95

137. 1926—"Pooh"   96

138. 1927—Lindbergh's Solo Atlantic Flight   97

139. 1927—Car Insurance   97

140. 1927—Execution of Sacco and Vanzetti   98

141. 1927—Babe Ruth Sets Home-Run Record   98

142. 1927—The First "Disc Jockey"   99

143. 1928—Herbert Hoover Elected President   100

144. 1928—"Steamboat Willie"   100

145. 1928—Antimatter   101

146. 1928—Academy Awards   101

147. 1929—The St. Valentine's Day Massacre   103

148. 1929—"Black Friday"   103

149. 1929—Byrd Flies Over South Pole   104

150. 1929—The Museum of Modern Art   105

151. 1930—The Ninth Planet Discovered   106

152. 1930—The Grand Slam of Golf   106

153. 1930—Population Explosion   107

154. 1930—The World Cup   107

155. 1931—A National Anthem   109

156. 1931—Nevada Legalizes Gambling   109

157. 1931—The Empire State Building   110

158. 1931—The British Commonwealth of Nations   111

159. 1932—Franklin D. Roosevelt Elected President   112

160. 1932—A Depression Anthem   112

161. 1932—Mobiles   113

162. 1932—Into the Stratosphere   113

163. 1933—The Concept of the Chain Reaction   114

164. 1933—"Fireside Chats"   115

165. 1933—*Ulysses* Allowed into United States   116

166. 1934—Hitler as Führer   117

167. 1934—The Long March   117

168. 1934—The Dust Bowl   118

169. 1935—National Labor Relations Act   119

170. 1935—Social Security   119

171. 1935—Joliot-Curies Win Nobel Prize in Chemistry   120

172. 1935—Alcoholics Anonymous   121

173. 1936—*Life* Magazine   122

174. 1936—Spanish Civil War   122

175. 1936—The "Nazi Olympics"   123

176. 1936—Abdication of Edward VIII of Great Britain   124

177. 1936—Roosevelt Reelected to Second Term   125

178. 1936—The Brotherhood of Sleeping Car Porters   125

179. 1937—Burning of the *Hindenburg*   127

180. 1937—Amelia Earhart Disappears in Pacific   127

181. 1938—Xeroxing   129

182. 1938—The House Un-American Activities
     Committee   129

183. 1938—"Peace in Our Time"   130

184. 1938—Polytetrafluorethylene   131

185. 1939—New York World's Fair   132

186. 1939—Hitler Invades Poland   132

187. 1939—Black Holes   133

188. 1939—Nylon Stockings   133

189. 1939—First Commercial Transatlantic Flight   134

190. 1939—Hollywood's Greatest Year   135

191. 1939—The Helicopter   135

192. 1940—The Retreat from Dunkirk   136

193. 1940—The Battle of Britain   136

194. 1940—Roosevelt Elected to Unprecedented Third
     Term   137

195. 1940—The Magnetron   138

196. 1940—Lend-Lease   138

197. 1940—The Blood Bank   139

198. 1941—The Siege of Leningrad   140

199. 1941—Marian Anderson Sings at the Lincoln
     Memorial   140

200. 1941—Mount Rushmore Memorial Completed   141

201. 1941—Mass Production of Penicillin   142

202. 1941—The Attack on Pearl Harbor   143

203. 1941—The United Nations   144

204. 1942—The "Final Solution"   145

205. 1942—Japanese Internment Camps in the United
     States   145

206. 1942—"I Shall Return"   146

207. 1942—The Battle of Midway   146

208. 1942—The Battle of Alamein   147

209. 1942—The Jeep   148

210. 1942—Controlled Chain Reaction   148

211. 1942—"Rosie the Riveter"   149

212. 1943—The Loss of a Star   151

213. 1943—The Pentagon   151

214. 1943—The Battle of Kursk   152

215. 1943—Superfortress B-29s   152

216. 1943—Italy Switches Sides   153

217. 1944—D-Day   154

218. 1944—The V-1 Rocket   155

219. 1944—Bretton Woods Conference   155

220. 1944—General de Gaulle Returns to Paris   156

221. 1944—Roosevelt Wins Fourth Term   156

222. 1945—American Flag Raised at Iwo Jima   158

223. 1945—Yalta   158

224. 1945—Hitler Commits Suicide   159

225. 1945—The European War Over   159

226. 1945—Potsdam Conference   160

227. 1945—Atomic Bomb Dropped on Hiroshima   161

228. 1946—The "Iron Curtain"   162

229. 1946—"Spock Says"   162

230. 1946—Nazi War Leaders Condemned to Death   163

231. 1946—ENIAC   163

232. 1947—The Marshall Plan   165

233. 1947—Jackie Robinson Breaks the Baseball Color
     Line   165

234. 1947—Partition of India and Pakistan 166

235. 1947—Breaking the Sound Barrier 167

236. 1947—Polaroid Camera 167

237. 1948—Gandhi Assassinated 169

238. 1948—The State of Israel Is Born 169

239. 1948—Apartheid Formalized 170

240. 1948—''Dewey Defeats Truman'' 171

241. 1948—The Long-Playing Record 171

242. 1949—The People's Republic of China 173

243. 1949—Radiocarbon Dating 173

244. 1949—National Basketball Association 174

245. 1950—First Organ Transplant 175

246. 1950—The Korean War Begins 175

247. 1950—The Diner's Club Card 176

248. 1950—Alger Hiss Convicted 176

249. 1951—Truman Fires MacArthur 178

250. 1952—Dick Button's Triple Jump 179

251. 1952—Dwight Eisenhower Elected President 179

252. 1952—Hydrogen Bomb 180

253. 1953—DNA 181

254. 1953—Everest Conquered 182

255. 1953—Coronation of Elizabeth II 182

256. 1953—Successful Impregnation with Frozen Sperm 183

257. 1954—Nuclear-Powered Submarine 184

258. 1954—Breaking the Four-Minute Mile 184

259. 1954—Polio Vaccine 185

260. 1954—Cigarettes Cause Cancer 185

261. 1954—Solar Batteries   186

262. 1954—Northland Shopping Mall   187

263. 1954—McCarthyism   188

264. 1956—Rosa Parks and the Montgomery Bus
Boycott   189

265. 1956—The Hungarian Uprising   190

266. 1956—Eisenhower Reelected   190

267. 1956—Television Remote Control   191

268. 1957—Civil Rights Act   192

269. 1959—Hawaii Becomes Fiftieth State   193

270. 1959—Castro's Cuba   193

271. 1959—De Gaulle and the Fifth Republic   194

272. 1960—Lasers   195

273. 1960—The Guggenheim Museum   195

274. 1960—First Televised Presidential Debates   196

275. 1960—John F. Kennedy Elected President   197

276. 1961—The "Military-Industrial Complex"   199

277. 1961—Yuri Gagarin Is First Man to Orbit Earth   199

278. 1961—Rudolf Nureyev Defects   200

279. 1961—The Berlin Wall Rises   201

280. 1961—The Peace Corps   201

281. 1962—John Glenn Is First American to Orbit Earth   202

282. 1962—*Silent Spring*   202

283. 1963—*The Feminine Mystique*   204

284. 1963—The March on Washington   204

285. 1963—President Kennedy Assassinated   205

286. 1964—The Beatles Come to America   206

287. 1964—*Ranger 7* Transmits Photos of Moon   206

288. 1964—Khrushchev Ousted as Soviet Leader 207

289. 1964—Warren Commission Report 207

290. 1964—Lyndon Johnson Wins Landslide Victory 208

291. 1965—Early Bird Communications Satellite 209

292. 1965—The Great Blackout 209

293. 1965—*Geminis* in Space Rendezvous 210

294. 1966—Draft Protests 211

295. 1966—Miranda Rights 211

296. 1966—The "Cultural Revolution" in China 212

297. 1967—Six-Day War in Middle East 213

298. 1967—Thurgood Marshall Becomes First Black on Supreme Court 213

299. 1967—First Heart Transplant 214

300. 1968—Martin Luther King, Jr., Assassinated 215

301. 1968—Robert F. Kennedy Assassinated 215

302. 1968—Richard M. Nixon Elected President 216

303. 1968—*Apollo* Astronauts Orbit Moon 216

304. 1969—Men Walk on Moon 217

305. 1970—Ozone Layer Warnings 218

306. 1971—Communist China Admitted to the United Nations 219

307. 1972—U.S./Soviet Arms Agreement 220

308. 1972—U.S. Supreme Court Bars Death Penalty 220

309. 1972—Equal Rights Amendment 221

310. 1972—Israeli Olympians Killed 221

311. 1972—Nixon Reelected in Landslide 222

312. 1973—Stephen Sondheim Ascendant 223

313. 1973—Vice President Agnew Resigns 224

314. 1974—President Nixon Resigns · 225

315. 1975—Watergate Conspirators Guilty · 226

316. 1975—Microsoft Founded · 226

317. 1976—*Viking 1* Lands on Mars · 228

318. 1976—Ordination of Women as Episcopal Priests · 228

319. 1976—Jimmy Carter Elected President · 229

320. 1977—Vietnam Draft Evaders Pardoned · 230

321. 1977—Panama Canal Treaty · 230

322. 1977—The *Gossamer Condor* · 231

323. 1978—John Paul II · 233

324. 1978—The Camp David Accords · 234

325. 1979—Three Mile Island Nuclear Accident · 235

326. 1979—Margaret Thatcher Becomes Prime Minister of Great Britain · 235

327. 1979—The Hostages in Iran · 236

328. 1980—The Walkman · 238

329. 1980—Microbes Can Be Patented · 238

330. 1980—Moscow Olympics Boycotted · 239

331. 1980—Ronald Reagan Elected President · 239

332. 1981—First Shuttle Flight · 240

333. 1981—Abortion Approved by Italian Voters · 241

334. 1981—AIDS Officially Recognized · 241

335. 1981—First Woman on Supreme Court · 242

336. 1982—"Pac-Man of the Year" · 243

337. 1983—*Pioneer 10* Leaves Solar System · 244

338. 1983—U.S. Loses America's Cup · 244

339. 1984—Torvill and Dean Find Perfection · 245

340. 1984—Home Video Taping Legal · 245

CONTENTS

341. 1984—Breakup of AT&T — 246

342. 1984—Reagan Reelected by Huge Margin — 246

343. 1985—Famine in Ethiopia — 248

344. 1986—Soviets Launch *Mir* Space Station — 249

345. 1986—Antiapartheid Act Passed by U.S. Congress — 249

346. 1988—The Grand Slam Plus — 251

347. 1988—George Bush Elected President — 251

348. 1989—The Berlin Wall Falls — 253

349. 1990—The Hubble Telescope — 254

350. 1990—Surgery on the Unborn — 254

351. 1990—Lech Walesa Elected President of Poland — 255

352. 1991—Pan American Airlines Closed Down — 256

353. 1991—"Operation Desert Storm" — 256

354. 1991—The End of the Soviet Union — 257

355. 1992—William Jefferson Clinton Elected President — 258

356. 1993—The Internet — 259

357. 1994—Election of Nelson Mandela — 260

358. 1995—The Oklahoma City Bombing — 261

359. 1996—Clinton Reelected President — 262

360. 1997—Dolly, a Cloned Sheep — 263

361. 1997—Death of Princess Diana — 263

362. 1998—Hong Kong Reverts to China — 265

363. 1998—Peace in Northern Ireland — 265

364. 1999—Impeachment of President Clinton — 267

365. 1999—The Millennium Bug — 268

THE 365 MOST IMPORTANT EVENTS

OF THE TWENTIETH CENTURY

INTRODUCTION

With two world wars and countless smaller conflicts, the twentieth century has been the bloodiest in human history. But it has also seen the spread of freedom around the world, with more representative democracies existing at the end of the century than ever before. Technological and medical breakthroughs have constantly turned science fiction into reality and greatly improved the lives of billions of people. New countries have been born, empires faded, and tyrannies brought down. And while technology has created its own potential threats, from nuclear war to global warming, the communications revolution and the birth of the Internet have given the human race a sense of interconnectedness never before known.

The story of the twentieth century has been so complex, across such an enormous range of human endeavors, that any attempt to capture its most important events means choosing among countless possibilities. The object of this book is to provide a perspective on the twentieth century by highlighting the events that have had lasting repercussions or influence. There are many events that create screaming headlines but fade with time. And there are events that receive little attention at first but in the end change the way millions of people live and think. Every decade has had its "trial of the century," in country after country, but while such circuses may fascinate when they occur, few bring about any real changes. They are of their moment and not much more. On the other side of the coin, an almost completely ignored scientific article or laboratory experiment can eventually alter the workings of the entire world. Thus this book covers not just the front-page stories that made military, political, scientific, and social history, but also spotlights many events that were less noted at the time yet went on to affect profoundly the shape of the twentieth century. You will find fewer entries in the 1980s and, particularly, the 1990s, simply because it is too soon to judge the real significance of many current events. Today's headline is not necessarily tomorrow's history.

No century can be understood simply in terms of great historical events. Archaeology has taught us that the shape of a spoon, a painting on the wall of a cave, or a bracelet can reveal much about the concerns and the daily lives of ancient peoples. Since we are defined as much by our tastes in music and literature, our sports enthusiasms, and our other leisure-time activities as by politics, these pages will also highlight the cultural landmarks, great sports achievements, and life-style developments that reveal the deeper nature of our lives.

As we enter the twenty-first century, we inevitably look back to see where we have come from, and what the events of the past one hundred years mean to the next one. *The 365 Most Important Events of the Twentieth Century* is intended to help in discovering some of the answers to such questions.

1.

1900—FIRST PICASSO EXHIBITION IN PARIS

As the new century was born, the nineteen-year-old Pablo Picasso, recently arrived in Paris from Spain, was given his first exhibition in the city whose art world he would come to lead. Arguably, other artists produced greater works that year, including Paul Cézanne, Henri Matisse, Edvard Munch, Claude Monet, Pierre Renoir, Henri Toulouse-Lautrec, and Auguste Rodin. They were all older and already celebrated, and Picasso's paintings of that year show the distinct influence of Lautrec. But beginning with the "Blue Period" paintings of 1901 and 1902, Picasso would rise to a level of fame and wealth unequaled by any other artist of the twentieth century.

2.

1900—WILLIAM MCKINLEY REELECTED

The 1900 election for president of the United States was a repeat of the 1896 election that pitted the Republican William McKinley against William Jennings Bryan. Bryan was one of the most important politicians ever to be defeated for the presidency. Although a religious fundamentalist, he was also in favor of women having the vote and the idea of the income tax. He advocated the adoption of "free silver" as an economic system rather than adherence to the gold standard. But McKinley was a widely loved man (despite the fact that his ill wife was one of the most disliked of all First Ladies), and at a time of great prosperity, he beat Bryan by a slightly larger margin than four years earlier, 292 electoral votes to 155.

3.

1900—CAMERAS FOR EVERYONE

In the first year of the new century, the Eastman Kodak Company introduced a camera that was cheap enough and simple enough to be used by anyone. In fact, advertisements specifically targeted youngsters: "Any school-boy or girl can make good pictures with one of the Eastman Kodak Co.'s Brownie Cameras." There were other small box cameras on the market by then, such as the Bullet, which cost $6, and the Buck-Eye, which cost $10. But the Brownie retailed for only $1, and a six-exposure film cartridge that could be loaded in daylight cost only 15 cents. A new market was tapped with the Brownie, marking the beginning of a century-long love affair with "family snapshots."

4.

1900—HAWAII AND PUERTO RICO BECOME
U.S. TERRITORIES

In the wake of the Spanish-American War (1898), the United States Congress declared Hawaii and Puerto Rico to be U.S. territories in separate bills on April 12 and April 30, 1900. Hawaii would become a key U.S. military base in the Pacific, whose importance led to the Japanese attack on Pearl Harbor in 1941, which brought the United States into World War II. Hawaii would also eventually become the fiftieth state as well as one of the most popular resort destinations for Americans. Puerto Ricans were granted U.S. citizenship in 1917, resulting in a considerable change in the demographics of the eastern United States.

5.

1900 — DISCOVERY OF THE MINOANS

In 1900, the English archeologist Arthur Evans discovered the remains of a previously unknown Bronze Age culture at Knossos on Crete. He named the culture Minoan after King Minos of Greek legend. It would eventually be revealed that the Minoans had flourished from 3000 to 1500 B.C., when the power center shifted to the Greek mainland, eventually giving rise to the Golden Age of Athens. Evans was knighted for his discovery, which added to our understanding of the complexity of Mediterranean history.

6.

1900 — PUBLICATION OF
THE WONDERFUL WIZARD OF OZ

The first of L. Frank Baum's fourteen Oz books was an immediate success when it appeared in 1900. Within three years, a musical version was playing on Broadway, and the show toured the country for years thereafter. Baum made several silent movies based on various Oz characters. *The Wizard of Oz*, the 1939 MGM movie musical starring Judy Garland, went on to become one of the most beloved American film classics. Baum's books are still hugely popular nearly a century later, and they are still dogged by surprising controversy. Almost every year throughout the century, somewhere in America, individuals or religious organizations have tried to remove the Oz books from public and school libraries on the grounds that they feature numerous examples of "witchcraft," incidents deemed corrupting to young souls. That the most popular of all

American stories for children should still be able to arouse controversy after nearly one hundred years in print says a great deal about the resilience of the urge to censor even in the freest of societies.

7.

1900—ART NOUVEAU SUBWAYS

The Art Nouveau movement had reached its apex in 1900, to the degree that Hector Guimard was commissioned to design entrances to the Paris Metro, or subway system, then being built. His enchanting wrought-iron designs were an essential part of the charm of Paris to generations of visitors and inhabitants, giving one the feeling of descending into some magical world rather than one of the world's first mass-transit systems. Art historians point out that no other movement in modern art met with such rapid public acceptance. The subway entrances of Hector Guimard were the ultimate example of this acceptance, integrating this mode of artistic expression into the daily lives of the humblest Parisian workers.

8.

1901—DEATH OF QUEEN VICTORIA

Born in 1819, Queen Victoria ascended the British throne at the age of eighteen in 1837, and ruled the British Empire with a firm hand for the next sixty-four years. Victoria gave her name to an age marked by fussy ornamental detail in clothing, furniture, and architecture, and by the rise of industrialism and the farthest extension of the empire in history, making her not only queen of Great Britain but also empress of India. The world had been changing rapidly in the last years of her reign, the longest in British history, and it would undergo seismic upheaval within a dozen years of her death. Her passing in 1901 marked not just the end of one century and the beginning of another, but a transition from one kind of world to another.

9.

1901—THE NOBEL PRIZES

Alfred Nobel, the Swedish chemist and munitions manufacturer who invented dynamite, had believed that his powerful explosives would bring an end to war. He was entirely wrong, of course, and to atone he created the Nobel Prizes, the most prestigious awards in the world. The first prizes—in chemistry, physics, physiology or medicine, literature, and peace—were awarded in 1901. An additional prize in economics was inaugurated in 1969. The prizes in the sciences, which often are awarded many years, even decades, after the discoveries they honor, have been relatively uncontroversial. However, there have always been strenuous arguments about the appropriateness of the more subjective literature and peace prizes. Among those who did not receive the literature prize, for instance, are such major figures as Henry James, Marcel Proust, and James Joyce. But it has been awarded to William Faulkner and Ernest Hemingway, along with seven other Americans.

10.

1901—THE ASSEMBLY LINE

The invention of the assembly line is often credited to automobile manufacturer Henry Ford, but the actual originator of this key industrial innovation was his great rival, Ransome E. Olds. Olds instituted the first assembly line in 1901, which enabled him to increase the output of his factory from 425 cars in 1901 to 2,500 in 1902. What Henry Ford did, in 1908, was to improve on Olds's idea by adding conveyor belts, which cut the time needed to manufacture his new Model-T from a day and a half to a mere ninety minutes.

11.

1901—"POMP AND CIRCUMSTANCE"

The British composer Sir Edward William Elgar (1857–1934) is still a concert favorite for such compositions as his Enigma Variations and Violin Concerto in B Minor. However, in 1901, he composed the first of a series of marches that have become among the most played pieces of music in the twentieth century. Elgar's "Pomp and Circumstance" marches have been played at school and college graduations to the extent that there can be few people in the Western world who have not heard them, whether they know the name of the composer or not.

12.

1902—BALLOT INITIATIVES

On June 2, 1902, America's first law permitting the public to instigate ballot initiatives, or referendums, was passed by the Oregon legislature. Most states would eventually allow such public initiatives, which require the gathering of a given number of signatures of registered voters. These referendums became much more common in the last two decades of the century, particularly in California, where they were often used to strike down existing laws. For example, Proposition 13, in 1978, rolled back property taxes, and Proposition 187, in 1994, designed to stop illegal immigrants from receiving nonemergency welfare, health services, or education, caused national debate. Oregon, always a progressive state, often passed referendums that extended public rights, as in 1994's Measure 16, which permitted euthanasia for the terminally ill in some circumstances.

13.

1902—CARUSO'S FIRST RECORDING

At the age of twenty-nine, the Italian tenor Enrico Caruso made his first recording at the Hotel di Milano, in that city, on March 18, 1902. Although he would die at forty-eight, and despite the technical crudeness of recording in the first two decades of the century, the beauty of his voice was such that he is still the mark by which all subsequent tenors have been measured. The bulk of his career was spent in America, where he sang at a total of seventeen annual opening nights at the Metropolitan Opera in New York City, a record that was finally equaled in 1998 by Plácido Domingo.

14.

1902 — HORMONES DISCOVERED

The existence and function of hormones were discovered by William Bayliss and Ernest Starling of Great Britain in 1902. The word "hormone" is derived from a Greek root that means "setting in motion." Hormones are chemical messengers, substances that are created by the endocrine glands. They are transported to a wide variety of tissues in the body, whose activities they regulate, either speeding them up or slowing them down. While human beings have particularly complex hormonal systems, they exist in all vertebrates and even in nonvertebrates, controling for example, the optic glands of the octopus. It has taken the entire twentieth century even to begin to unravel the complexities of hormonal messages, and of related chemical messengers like pheronomes, which signal sexual attraction in many animal and insect species. Hormones have come to play a significant role in modern medicine, one that is likely to grow in the next century.

15.

1902 — JUST SO STORIES

Although 1902 saw the publication of such great works of literature as *The Wings of the Dove*, by Henry James, *The Heart of Darkness*, by Joseph Conrad, and *The Immoralist*, by André Gide, the most widely read book then and since that was offered to the public that year is undoubtedly Rudyard Kipling's *Just So Stories*. Millions of children over the past hundred years have been enthralled by "How the Elephant Got Its Trunk," and "How the Leopard Got Its

Spots." As stage productions, movies, and television series, these stories have stretched the imaginations of children, and have found a special spot in their memories for generations.

16.

1902—THE ROSE BOWL

The first Rose Bowl game in 1902 was the start of the American mania with football. The initial game was won by Michigan over Stanford by a score of 49–0. Both teams have played in many other Rose Bowls since. The Rose Bowl Parade, a fixture on television since the 1950s, is the most watched parade in America except for the Macy's Thanksgiving Day Parade. The success of the Rose Bowl on television was enormous, and led to a proliferation of bowl games in the second half of the century. There are now so many that they must be played over a period of three days from December 31 to January 2, but the New Year's Day Rose Bowl extravaganza remains the most popular.

17.

1902—*THE THREE SISTERS*

The third of Anton Chekhov's plays to be produced at the Moscow Art Theater to wide acclaim, and the first in the twentieth century, *The Three Sisters* remains the most often presented of his plays, even more than *Uncle Vanya* in 1899. It is regarded as one of the supreme tests of actors and directors, who must capture both its despair and its humor. Although two earlier Chekhov plays had been given revivals at the Moscow Art Theater, *The Three Sisters* was the first to be developed from scratch, according to the theories of the theater's director, Constantin Stanislavsky. His teachings gave rise to "Method" acting in America, and *The Three Sisters* remains a touchstone for the Actor's Studio in New York City. *The Three Sisters* also forms an integral part of the training of many of America's and Russia's most noted actresses.

18.

1903 — THE FLYING MACHINE

Humankind's most ancient dream of flying through the air, expressed in the Greek myth of Icarus, the drawings of Leonardo da Vinci, and on through the balloon flights of the nineteenth century, had still not been achieved in a powered machine as the twentieth century began. Even though numerous inventors had tried to build such a machine, and the gas engine had existed since 1859, many "experts" still believed that powered flight controlled by an on-board pilot was impossible. But on December 17, 1903, two brothers—bicycle shop owners and inventors from Dayton, Ohio— achieved the dream on the beach at Kitty Hawk, North Carolina.

Orville and Wilbur Wright's machine had wings controlled by movable parts, a crucial advance, and on that day in 1903 they made four flights. Orville's was the first, but Wilbur flew the fourth and longest effort, which covered 852 feet and lasted just under a minute. In the third year of the twentieth century a new age was born, on a beach by the sea, in a handmade flying machine.

19.

1903 — FIRST PRIMARY ELECTIONS

Wisconsin, always a progressive state, became the first in the union to hold primary elections for political office in 1903, in order to give citizens a larger say in picking candidates. While the rule of the party bosses continued for decades in many states, primaries eventually became the rule across the country. Because of the primary system, many political unknowns have been able to get on ballots at all levels of government, often displacing chosen party stalwarts. The result has been strengthening of democratic choice and a diminishment of party rule.

20.

1903—A MESSAGE SENT AROUND THE WORLD

On July 4, 1903, President Theodore Roosevelt inaugurated the new Pacific Ocean communications cable by sending a greeting around the entire globe. That day can be seen as the beginning of the creation of what Marshall McLuhan would call, more than sixty years later, "The Global Village." The first two fully successful transatlantic cables had been laid under the Atlantic Ocean in 1866. Many others followed, both under the Atlantic and other seas around the world. But it was not until 1903 that it became possible to send a message that circumnavigated the globe.

21.

1903—THE WORLD SERIES

In the autumn of 1903, the Boston Red Sox of the upstart American League beat the Pittsburgh Pirates of the National League in a single game by a score of 5–3. This initial encounter between the two leagues would grow into an annual "fall classic" that has been at the center of American sports ever since. The annual football Super Bowl, because it is still limited to a single game, draws more viewers, but the World Series, which can stretch to seven games, retains a special mystique. The proliferation of other televised sports—particularly basketball and, to a lesser extent, hockey—has cut into the baseball and football fan base to some degree, but to millions of Americans the can-you-top-this recitation of World Series statistics and lore remains a central form of American armchair and barstool competition.

22.

1903—THE TOUR DE FRANCE

An Italian chimney sweep named Maurice Garin won the first Tour de France bicycle race in 1903. The annual race, which takes place in July and August, has a different route each year and it sometimes passes through neighboring countries as well, but its finish line is always in Paris. Lasting four grueling weeks, the Tour de France has been regarded almost from the beginning as one of Europe's most important sporting events, but it did not attract widespread American attention until Greg LeMond of the United States captured the first of four victories in 1986. Cycling has grown greatly in popularity in the United States since then, and in the past three Olympics there have been several Americans in serious contention, as has also been the case in the Tour de France. Major races now take place annually in most American cities, large and small.

23.

1903—THE HARLEY-DAVIDSON MOTORCYCLE

The first Harley-Davidson motorcycle was built by William Harley and the three Davidson brothers when the early automobiles were still regarded by most Americans as chiefly designed to "frighten horses." Automobiles would completely change the face of the planet, but motorcycles would grow steadily in popularity as

15

well. Associated with gangs like the Hell's Angels, as reflected by the 1954 movie *The Wild One,* starring Marlon Brando, or viewed as a vehicle for the outsider, as in Dennis Hopper's classic *Easy Rider* of 1969, motorcycles have steadily become more mainstream. When 200,000 motorcyclists gather in Daytona Beach, Florida, for Motorcycle Week each year, the majority of the assembled owners are professional people—doctors, lawyers, stockbrokers, and the like. And to this day, a Harley-Davidson motorcycle is regarded as the ultimate machine.

24.

1904 — HELEN KELLER GRADUATES FROM RADCLIFFE COLLEGE

Born in 1880, deaf and blind from the age of two, Helen Keller was put in the hands of a special teacher, Annie Sullivan, at the age of seven. Sullivan, using pioneering methods, managed to reach Keller in her dark, silent world and unleash the great intelligence that resided there. Keller was twenty-four when she graduated from Radcliffe College. Her success in overcoming her problems had an incalculable effect on public attitudes toward the handicapped. She ultimately mastered several languages, and lectured worldwide to raise funds for the education of the blind. Her story, as told in her autobiography and other books, helped pave the way for better lives for millions of people in the course of the twentieth century.

25.

1904 — YELLOW FEVER CONTROL

The building of the Panama Canal began in 1904, and from the start workers in large numbers contracted yellow fever, which in many cases resulted in coma and death. The United States Surgeon General, William Crawford Gorgas, was sent to deal with the problem. Gorgas had been a physician with the Army Medical Corps since 1880, and had himself survived yellow fever, making him immune. In 1898, acting on the the surgeon Walter Reed's discovery that yellow fever was carried by a particular species of mosquito, he had experimented with combating the disease through mosquito control in Havana, Cuba, and met with marked success. But this approach was so new and so costly that it took the personal intervention of President Theodore Roosevelt to acquire the funds necessary to carrying out such a program in the Canal Zone. Since the building of the canal was followed with intense interest throughout the world, Gorgas's success in eventually controlling yellow fever and malaria, also carried by mosquitos, was reported around the globe. His methods were no longer regarded as "experimental" and were adopted internationally.

26.

1904—THE TEA BAG

As though the British were not already convinced that their former colonies, now well into their second century as the United States of America, were beyond redemption, in 1904, an American came up with a new invention he called the tea bag. Thomas Sullivan knew that get-up-and-go Americans couldn't be bothered with the British ritual of brewing loose tea leaves in a pot. So he decided to put the leaves in a porous bag that could be put into a cup and pulled out again in a couple of minutes without leaving any nasty residue. His invention never quite managed to persuade Americans to abandon their love of coffee, but it became the most common way to brew tea around the world, even, after a few decades, in the British Isles.

27.

1904—SAFETY RAZOR BLADES

Early ads for safety razors and blades suggested that they were fit for a king. In fact, they had been invented by one—so to speak. In 1904, the patent on the safety razor was taken out by the

American inventor King Camp Gillette. Within two years, ninety thousand of his razors and twelve million of the replaceable blades were being sold annually, figures that would continue to rise as the smooth-shaven face became the standard fashion. The first of Gillette's razors had silver- or gold-plated handles, but even today's disposable plastic razors are closely related to his original design.

28.

1904—FIRST AMERICAN SUBWAY

The first true subway line, offering speedy mass transit for the working classes, opened in New York City in 1904. The initial Broadway Line, running from City Hall to 145th Street in Harlem would be supplemented by many additional lines in the years to come, uniting all the city's boroughs except Staten Island, long reachable only by ferry and later by bridge as well. No other American city would build as extensive a subway system as New York, but London, Paris, and Tokyo have systems on a comparable scale, while many other cities around the world have lesser ones.

29.

1904—*THE GREAT TRAIN ROBBERY*

Thomas Edison produced the first popular American film with a story, *The Great Train Robbery*, a fourteen-minute narrative. The movie, completed in 1904, was the opening event at America's first true movie theater, in Pittsburgh, Pennsylvania, the following year. In terms of the development of movies as an art form, the most important aspect of *The Great Train Robbery*, aside from the fact that it had a story line, was its editing. The Edison Company cameraman and editor, Edwin S. Porter, spliced pieces of film together to give rhythm and variety to the visual elements. Although Porter's editing was largely intuitive, it laid the foundation for the development of the modern film with its closeups and long shots, and its ever more sophisticated use of cutting between elements within a scene, and between different scenes.

30.

1904—THEODORE ROOSEVELT WINS LANDSLIDE VICTORY

Having becoming president in 1901 following the assassination of President William McKinley, Theodore Roosevelt had undercut the Democrats by becoming a "trustbuster" and campaigning against "big money." He and his wife Edith's large, rambunctious family were very popular occupants of the White House. He won a huge victory in November 1904 over the lackluster Democratic candidate, Judge Alton B. Parker of New York, winning every state outside the South and garnering 336 electoral votes to Parker's 140.

31.

1904—THE ST. LOUIS EXPOSITION

The first World's Fair of the twentieth century was the St. Louis Exposition. The fair is probably best known to devotees of the Judy Garland movie *Meet Me in St. Louis,* in which she introduced the famous "Trolley Song." The actual fair also had a profound effect on American eating habits. German immigrants from Hamburg decided to cater to the American love for sandwiches, and put a beef patty between two halves of a bun. With visitors from all over the country attending the fair, this new culinary creation became available everywhere in a very short time. The ice cream cone was also popularized at the fair, although there are those who claim that it had already gotten a start in New York City.

32.

1904—*MADAMA BUTTERFLY*

Giacomo Puccini's *Madama Butterfly*, which premiered in 1904, has proved the most popular opera composed in this century. His even more beloved *La Bohème* had its first performance in 1896. *Madama Butterfly* was based on a play by David Belasco and J. L. Long that was a Broadway hit in 1900; another Belasco play would provide the basis for Puccini's later opera *The Girl of the Golden West*. *Butterfly* is in the repertoire of almost every major opera house in the world, and has been the signature role for many of the century's great sopranos. Its sentimentally tragic story and lush melodies have proved so endlessly appealing that it is sometimes blamed for audience resistance to musically and emotionally harder-edged modern operas.

33.

1904—*PETER PAN*

The boy who refused to grow up, Peter Pan, was created by Sir J. M. Barrie, a Scottish playwright and novelist who also wrote such well-known plays as *The Admirable Crichton* and *What Every Woman Knows*. Peter Pan; his mischievous fairy cohort, Tinkerbell;

the ominous Captain Cook; Nana, the faithful dog of the Darling family; the Darling children, particularly Wendy, and of course, Captain Hook's nemesis, the tick-tocking crocodile, have always had a special place in the hearts of children of all ages. Like Oz, Never Land is a place all children would like to visit.

34.

1905—U.S. ARMY SUBMARINES

The first practical submarine, called the *Turtle*, had been built by a Yale undergraduate in 1776, and was dubbed by George Washington an "effort of genius." Although many submarines would be built over the next 125 years, they had many problems, and it was not until 1900 that John P. Holland, an Irish immigrant to the United States, built a vessel that could pass rigorous tests. This design, dubbed Class A, was propelled by a gasoline engine while on the surface of the sea, and by an electric motor when submerged. Capable of traversing 1,500 miles, it had a conning tower and tanks with reserve fresh air. After the U.S. Army began to build Class A submarines in 1905, they quickly became the standard around the world. A new element had been introduced into warfare.

35.

1905—NOVOCAINE

The local anesthetic novocaine was invented in 1905 by the German surgeon H. F. W. Braun. It became the most widely used pain-killer in the practice of dentistry, blotting out the pain if not the noise of the drill, and thus encouraging the idea of the regular dental checkup. Lidocaine, a similar anesthetic, was introduced later, and gas mixtures that produce a semiconscious state have also been widely used in dentistry in recent decades. However, novocaine remains one of the most successful anesthetics ever invented.

36.

1905—THE MERRY WIDOW

The Hungarian composer Franz Lehar premiered his operetta *The Merry Widow* in 1905. Its frothy story and lilting melodies made it not only an immediate hit but the most successful work of its kind in the twentieth century. While technically an operetta rather than a full-scale opera, it has been a standard at opera houses around the world because the title role offers coloratura sopranos the perfect vehicle for engaging singing that is less taxing than most of the opera repertoire.

37.

1905—THE AUDUBON SOCIETY

Huge hats with huge feathers stuck in them were all the rage just after the the turn of the century. And exotic birds were being slaughtered by the hundreds of thousands to provide those feathers. There had been a movement to preserve land and wildlife since the middle of the nineteenth century, but it received new support from the conservationist concerns of President Theodore Roosevelt. One of the results was the formation of the Audubon Society. The society was named for the great American ornithologist and painter of birds John James Audubon, who had arrived in America from what is now Haiti in 1803, and who over the next several decades produced absolutely correct pictorial studies of birds that have been called "one of the great achievements of American intellectual history." The paintings were also extremely beautiful and widely published in many editions. The Audubon Society has had an incalculable effect on the American conservation movement since its founding. It is especially appropriate to the American story that the genius for whom it was named was of mixed white and African heritage.

38.

1906—A NEW FORMULA FOR COCA-COLA

Although the company long denied it, ample documentation has shown that the original formula for Coca-Cola contained a small amount of cocaine. In 1906, however, the formula was changed and caffeine was substituted for the cocaine. Those who were born in the 1890s and drank the old formula as children noticed that the drink didn't have quite the same kick after 1905, but the change was clearly a judicious one, since Coca-Cola went on to become the century's most popular soft drink.

39.

1906—THE FORWARD PASS

We all have our priorities, and among sports fans one of the most important events of the century was undoubtedly the change in rules by the Intercollegiate Athletic Association in 1906 that allowed the use of the forward pass in football. Before that time, American football was largely a running game, with only lateral passes permitted. It is extremely doubtful that there would be a Super Bowl if the forward pass had remained illegal.

40.

1906—SAN FRANCISCO EARTHQUAKE

Before dawn on April 18, 1906, San Francisco, California, was rocked by what became known as the Great Earthquake. While the quake destroyed many buildings, it was the fire that followed that did the greatest damage as it burned in some areas for days.

The great opera singer Enrico Caruso had performed the previous night, and after barely escaping his hotel before it collapsed, vowed never again to return to California. A young Italian-American banker named Amadeo Giannini hauled his bank's $80,000 in gold out of town on a vegetable cart, and then set up business on Washington Wharf, where he operated from a plank placed between two barrels. Giannini made loans to anyone who asked, provided their hands were calloused, this form of "collateral" proving to him that they were honest workingmen. He became a San Francisco legend, and succeeded in building his banking empire to the point that it became the Bank of America, the country's largest banking institution. San Francisco itself was quickly rebuilt, pioneering the use of "earthquake proof" construction methods that would subsequently be adopted around the world in quake zones.

41.

1907—THE ELECTRIC WASHING MACHINE

The Hurley Machine Company of Chicago, Illinois, began marketing the first electric washing machines in 1907. They would only gradually gain favor, although there was a spurt in sales following rural electrification efforts by the federal government in the 1930s. Following World War II, electric washing machines became an essential appliance for new housing at the start of the baby-boom years.

42.

1907—CONSERVATION

President Theodore Roosevelt's seventh annual message to the United States Congress (what would later become the State of the Union address) was the first ever to emphasize conservation. A great sportsman, Teddy Roosevelt gave enormous impetus to the conservation movement in the United States. During his tenure, the first national bird sanctuary, Florida's Pelican Island, was created, and 148 million acres of land were set aside as national forests. He also pushed Congress to create such national parks as Crater Lake in Oregon, Petrified Forest in Arizona, and Wind Cave in South Dakota. In this he was following in the footsteps of his party's first president, Abraham Lincoln, who initiated the creation of Yellowstone National Park, which was finally approved by Congress in 1872.

43.

1907—DAILY COMIC STRIP

While cartoons, especially political ones, had been featured in newspapers as far back as the American Revolution, strip cartoons, telling miniature stories about recurring characters, are a twentieth-century development. The first comic strip to appear on a daily basis began life in the *San Francisco Chronicle* in 1907. Drawn by Bud Fisher, it was called "Mr. Mutt," but soon its name changed to "Mutt and Jeff," and as its popularity soared across the country, it was joined by numerous other strips. "The Funnies" became an integral part of most daily newspapers in the United States—although never the august *New York Times*.

44.

1907—CORPORATE CAMPAIGN
CONTRIBUTIONS OUTLAWED

Way back in 1907, the United States Congress decided to grit its teeth and ban political contributions by corporations. Such controls over campaign contributions have been an on-again, off-again story for the remainder of the century, and many of the same arguments, on both sides, that were noisily expressed on this issue in the late 1990s could be heard back in 1907. Some things never change.

45.

1908—THE MODEL-T

As his company introduced its new Model-T car in 1908, Henry Ford said, "I am going to democratize the automobile, and when I'm through, everybody will, be able to afford one, and about everybody will have one." The first Model-Ts sold for $850, and the price got lower every year until it reached $290 in 1923. Between 1908 and 1927, 15.8 million Model-Ts were sold, but they finally went out of favor because Ford stubbornly refused to sell them in any color but black, and insisted on keeping the gas tank under the front seat, which meant that a cushion had to be moved to fill up the tank.

46.

1908—WILLIAM H. TAFT IS ELECTED

William H. Taft served as President Theodore Roosevelt's secretary of war from 1904 to 1908, and was handpicked by Roosevelt as his successor. Easily nominated by the Republicans with such backing, he was opposed by William J. Bryan, whose third Democratic nomination it was. Bryan ran his least successful campaign, and Taft was elected president by 321 electoral votes to 162. Taft was the largest president in U.S. history, weighing well over three hundred pounds, and a special bathtub had to be installed for him in the White House. His presidency was not a successful one, but he was subsequently appointed Chief Justice of the United States Supreme Court by President Warren G. Harding, serving in that office from 1921 to 1930.

47.

1909—FREUD VISITS AMERICA

In September 1909, Sigmund Freud came to the United States to deliver a series of lectures at Clark University in Massachusetts. Clark was a relatively small educational institution that in the early part of the century was on the cutting edge in several academic fields. Freud's work had until recently been largely disparaged in Europe, but he was given a warm welcome in the States, and many important American intellectual figures, including the American philosopher William James, came from all over to hear his lectures. This visit to America set in motion a widespread enthusiasm for psychoanalytic ideas in the United States, where they were to become particularly important to social and cultural developments. Ironically, Freud disliked America intensely and never returned to the country that ensured the wide influence of his ideas.

48.

1 9 1 0 — M A R I E   C U R I E   I S O L A T E S   R A D I U M

In 1903, Marie Curie, her husband, Pierre, and Antoine Becquerel had received the Nobel Prize in Physics for their work on radioactivity. In 1910, Marie Curie finally succeeded in isolating the radioactive element radium, although she and her husband had confirmed its existence in 1904. She was awarded the Nobel Prize in Chemistry the following year, the first person to win two Nobel Prizes, the first to win in two different categories, and the only woman to do so to this day. Her husband, who was twelve years older, had died in 1906 at the age of forty-seven, while Marie developed leukemia because of her constant exposure to radiation and died in 1934.

49.

1 9 1 0 — T H E   B O Y   S C O U T S

Sir Robert Baden-Powell founded the original Boy Scouts in Great Britain in 1908; its American counterpart was incorporated in 1910. Open to boys from seven to eighteen years of age, the Boy Scout movement stressed mental, moral, and physical development. Outdoor skills, lifesaving techniques, and training in good citizenship offered young members the opportunity to acquire a successive series of merit badges. In the course of the century, more than a hundred million American boys have been members of the Boy Scouts.

50.

1910—THE RETURN OF HALLEY'S COMET

In 1682, Edmund Halley had been mesmerized by the great comet that appeared that year. Shortly afterward, he became involved in editing and paying for the publication of Sir Isaac Newton's great work on gravity. Newton's revolutionary calculations of the effects of gravity on the orbit of the planets gave Halley the information he needed to predict, correctly, that the great comet would appear again in 1759, and every seventy-five or seventy-six years thereafter. The comet arrived on schedule in 1910, but as a result of fantastic speculations by the French astronomer Camille Flammarion, a public panic developed. Flammarion had said that cyanogen, a poisonous gas in the comet's tail, might wipe out all life on Earth because of the comet's very close approach to the planet. Several cities around the world, and particularly Chicago in the United States, were gripped by hysteria despite the efforts of other scientists to dispel such utterly misplaced alarms.

Ancient societies had often been deeply alarmed by comets and eclipses, but the events of 1910 showed that even a "modern" society could be affected by these phenomena. Indeed, even at the end of the century there are those who believe the "end of the world" predictions of such figures as Pat Robertson—although he always seems to be able to avert disaster through prayer. The second twentieth-century return of the comet, in March 1986, caused not panic but disappointment, since on this occasion it was too far away to produce much of a show.

51.

1910—EQUAL BILLING FOR BLACK PERFORMER

In 1910, the black song-and-dance phenomenon Bert Williams joined the Ziegfeld Follies, Broadway's top-drawing revue, famous for its lavish sets and costumes, long-legged showgirls, and major stars, including such luminaries as Will Rogers and Fanny Brice over the years. Williams was a talent of such magnitude that he was accorded equal billing with the white stars of the show—a first for a black entertainer. Williams thus became an early exemplar of one of the main routes to integration for American blacks: show business. In those days, of course, Williams could not stay in the same hotels or eat in the same restaurants as white members of the cast, but the equal billing he achieved was a major breakthrough at the time.

52.

1910—MOUNT WILSON TELESCOPE

Born in 1878 to an extremely wealthy Chicago family, George Ellery Hale had a brilliant mind and the social connections to raise huge sums of money for scientific and educational projects. He had established a reputation as an astronomer by the time he was twenty-three, taking the first photographs of solar flares. In 1903, he climbed Mount Wilson, near Pasadena, California, and at its six-thousand-foot summit he looked up at the night sky through the crystalline air and decided to build the world's greatest observatory. With the help of such donors as Andrew Carnegie, who alone provided $10 million, the 2.54m/100-inch reflecting telescope was completed in 1910. It became one of the world's most important scientific centers. Albert Einstein's first trip to America was made specifically to study the data being amassed at the Mount Wilson Observatory. George Hale, who was also one of the founders of the California Institute of Technology, is little remembered by the general public, but in the scientific community his vision and ability to make his ideas reality mark him as one of the most important contributors to the advancement of twentieth-century science.

53.

1911—ADOPTION OF GREENWICH MEAN TIME

At midnight on March 10–11, 1911, France and its colony Algeria turned their clocks back by nine minutes and twenty-one seconds. In so doing, after long resistance, France accepted the Greenwich standard of solar time, as measured at the former Royal Observatory in Greenwich, England. In years to come, holdouts in the Middle East and Asia would accept the Greenwich standard, putting the entire planet on the same wavelength. There are still numerous specialized calendars by which holidays are determined, including Jewish, Eastern Orthodox, and Chinese, but the entire world operates by a single measurement of daily time—Greenwich Mean Time.

54.

1911—AMUNDSEN REACHES THE SOUTH POLE

The Norwegian explorer Roald Amundsen was the first to reach the South Pole, in 1911. In 1903–1906, he had also commanded the first single ship to sail through the Northwest Passage, the water route between the Atlantic and Pacific oceans in the subpolar region. He would also be the first to fly over the North Pole in 1926, together with the aviator Alberto Nobile and the financier Lincoln Ellsworth. He was killed trying to rescue Nobile from a crash in the Arctic in 1928.

55.

1911—RUPERT BROOKE'S *POEMS*

At the age of twenty-four, the British poet Rupert Brooke published a volume of collected poems, including such master-
pieces as "Grantchester," and became the darling of the English
literary world. Byronically handsome, but with a much happier personality than Byron, he was one of many young Englishmen who
went off to fight in World War I with a patriotic flourish, but his
sonnet "The Soldier" seemed to foretell his own death. When he
did indeed meet a tragic death in 1915, he became a legend in Great
Britain, a symbol of all the young lives snuffed out in that futile
war, in which a generation of his country's best and brightest were
lost.

56.

1911—TRAFFIC CONTROL

With Henry Ford's Model-T and other automobiles selling as
fast as Detroit could turn them out, a citizen of Trenton,
Michigan, named Edward Hines hand-painted white lines on the
main street of his town to indicate traffic lanes. Three years later,
on August 5, 1914, the world's first traffic light, utilizing the fa-
miliar red and green, was installed in Cleveland, Ohio, at the corner
of Euclid Avenue and East 105th Street.

57.

1911—STANDARD OIL IS BROKEN UP

The holding company Standard Oil, formed in New Jersey in 1899 by the most famous of the "robber barons" of the late nineteenth century, John D. Rockefeller, was created to get around new regulatory statutes aimed at the monopolistic practices of the more than seventy-five companies Rockefeller controlled. These companies produced 90 percent of the oil in the United States, refined it, distributed it, and sold it to the public. But in 1911, Standard Oil of New Jersey was ordered dissolved by the U.S. Supreme Court, under provisions of the Sherman Antitrust Act of 1890, following a decade of litigation by the U.S. Justice Department. Rockefeller himself was by then merely a figurehead, and had begun rescuing his family name by dispensing vast funds to charity, establishing the Rockefeller Foundation, restoring Colonial Williamsburg, and founding New York City's Riverside Church. The breakup of Standard Oil was the precursor to such antitrust actions as the breakup of Bell Telephone in the 1980s and the 1998 antitrust suit against Microsoft.

58.

1911—DER ROSENKAVALIER

The German composer Richard Strauss was already famous for his tone poems *Death and Transfiguration* (1889) and *Thus Spake Zarathustra* (1895) when he turned to writing operas. *Salomé* (1905) and *Elektra* (1909) were regarded as important works, but it was not until *Der Rosenkavalier,* which premiered on January 26, 1911, at England's Royal Opera House, that he achieved huge popular success as an opera composer. The libretto for *Der Rosenkavalier* was written by the Austrian dramatist and poet Hugo von Hofmannsthal, who had also been the librettist for *Elektra* and would be for *Ariadne auf Naxos*, Strauss's opera of 1912. The role of the aging Marschallin in *Der Rosenkavalier*, who loses her young lover Count Octavian (a "pants" role sung by a mezzo-soprano) to Sophie von Faninal, is one of the most famous of all soprano roles, and has been given extraordinary dimension by such great singers as Elizabeth Schwarzkopf and Kiri Te Kanawa. The opera's final trio, sung by the three central characters, is regarded by many music lovers as the most beautiful music ever written for the human voice.

59.

1912—THE SOS DISTRESS CODE

In 1912, the SOS distress signal, to be tapped out in Morse code on the telegraph, was accepted as a universal call for help by ships at sea. One of its first uses was by the *Titanic*, which sent out the signal after striking an iceberg on April 14, 1912. Despite the massive loss of life in that disaster, the use of the code did bring crucial help from the *Carpathia*, which steamed to the rescue and picked up those who had been able to find places in the insufficient number of lifeboats. The SOS code was subsequently responsible for saving untold thousands of lives at sea. Computerized telecommunications through satellites have largely replaced the use of Morse code in the last two decades, but for seventy years the SOS signal was the last best hope of countless foundering ships of all sizes.

60.

1912—PARACHUTING

Albert Berry of the United States became the first man to use a parachute to jump from an airplane on March 1, 1912. The parachute would become a fundamental safety device for pilots and other crew members of airplanes. In World War II, massive parachute drops from B-52s and other large planes would deliver hundreds of thousands of soldiers to the front lines of battle. Parachuting would also become a popular sport. Former President George Bush, who had parachuted to safety from his damaged plane during World War II in the Pacific, made a pleasure jump at the age of seventy-three in 1997.

61.

1912—THE CONCEPT OF
CONTINENTAL DRIFT

In 1912, the German geologist Alfred Wegener first suggested that the existing continents had originally formed a single, enormous land mass that he named Pangea, from the Greek for "all earth." In 1915, Wegener published a major paper on the subject, showing how that land mass had broken apart, with the smaller masses drifting to their present positions as the continents we know. His idea was based on a revolutionary concept: that the land masses were always in motion, even if it was difficult for us to perceive the fact, carried on thin tectonic plates on the surface of the earth. Although it was not until the 1980s that hard geological evidence proved Wegener's idea of a previous single supercontinent, his theories were fundamental to an entirely new understanding of the nature of the earth, one that greatly assisted scientists in the study of earthquakes, volcanoes, mountain ranges, and many other geological features.

62.

1912—THE CONSUMER PRICE INDEX

The Consumer Price Index (CPI), which measures the goods and services bought by a typical American family, has played a part in determining the size of the paycheck of millions of Americans since it was first used in 1912. Initially serving as a guide to cost-of-living adjustments for wage earners, particularly union members, the CPI ultimately came to affect Social Security payments and numerous other economic entities. To this day it remains one of the most important guideposts to the performance of the American economy, a crucial barometer of inflation. Not only does it figure in the decisions made by the Federal Reserve Board when setting interest rates for the nation's banks, but also can raise or lower Social Security payments, which are directly linked to the inflation it measures.

63.

1912—WOODROW WILSON ELECTED PRESIDENT

During his four-year term, President Taft had turned his back on many of the reforms of his mentor, Teddy Roosevelt. A furious Roosevelt founded his own party, the Bull Moose Party, and ran again, thus ensuring the election of Woodrow Wilson, the former president of Princeton University and governor of New Jersey. Wilson became the first Democrat elected in the twentieth century, and only the second since 1856; Grover Cleveland had been elected to two nonsequential terms, in 1884 and 1892. Wilson won a whopping 435 electoral votes, with Roosevelt coming in second with 88, while Taft won only 8, those of Utah and Vermont. The popular vote told a different story, with Wilson getting just under 42 percent, Roosevelt 27 percent, and Taft 23 percent.

64.

1912—PILTDOWN MAN, THE ''MISSING LINK''

Charles Dawson, a British lawyer and keen amateur geologist, discovered a skull in a gravel bed on Piltdown Common near Lewes, England, in 1912. The skull combined a clearly human cranium with an apelike jaw. Nothing like it had been discovered before, and it was soon acclaimed as belonging to the "missing link" between apes and early human beings. Major scientists attested to the authenticity of the skull, and it was duly covered in school textbooks. There had always been skeptics about Piltdown Man who asked why no other bones were found at the site and why no other such skull had ever turned up. But for forty years, its authenticity was widely accepted. Eventually, however, new chemical tests were used on the skull, and in 1953 it was revealed to be a hoax. A human cranium had been attached to an orangutan's jaw with great precision, and the whole treated to make it appear ancient. It would take another forty-three years, the eventual discovery of an old trunk at the British Museum, and much detective work to reveal the identity of the perpetrator of the hoax. It turned out to be a man named M. A. Hinton, who had been treated badly at the British Museum as a young man, although he eventually became its keeper of zoology in the 1930s. His hoax had been an all-too-successful attempt to embarrass the museum, but as he became more prominent himself, it had been increasingly difficult to admit what he had done. The twentieth century has had many scientific hoaxes, but Piltdown Man was the most successful.

65.

1912—MASSACHUSETTS SETS MINIMUM WAGE

The idea of the minimum wage had first been introduced in New Zealand in 1894, but Massachusetts was the first state to adopt such a code in America. It was subsequently passed by many additional states, and became federal law in 1938 with the passage of the Fair Labor Standards Act. The minimum wage has steadily risen ever since, although there have always been opponents in the business world to say that an additional rise would bankrupt them.

66.

1912—HOLLYWOOD STUDIOS

In 1912, three of the most important Hollywood studios were born: Warner Brothers, Fox Studios (later Twentieth Century-Fox), and Universal Studios. While these companies would undergo many changes over the next decade, they all made their first short subjects in 1912. Along with Paramount Pictures and Metro-Goldwyn-Mayer, amalgamated from three smaller studios in 1924, the original three studios would become the backbone of the twentieth century's signature form of popular entertainment and, at its best, artistic achievement. Despite many ups and downs, all of these studios still function in some form to this day, even if largely as financial backers and distributors of projects initiated by individual stars or directors.

67.

1912—THE KEYSTONE COMEDIES

In 1912, Mack Sennett, who had starred in and then directed many short films for D. W. Griffith's Biograph Films, started his own small studio, called Keystone. Keystone would become the greatest exponent of the slapstick-comedy film in the silent era. Charlie Chaplin began his movie career at Keystone, and other stars who made their mark with the studio included Buster Keaton, Fatty Arbuckle, Mabel Norman, Chester Conklin, and many others. The Keystone Kops were a particular favorite with the public, which couldn't seem to get enough of the antics of these incompetent lawmen.

68.

1913—INCOME TAXES

Although rulers have collected taxes on income since biblical times, it was not until the end of the eighteenth century that the modern income tax came into being, when Great Britain levied one to help finance the Napoleonic wars. The American Civil War brought into being a similar tax, but it was not until 1913 that the income tax became a permanent fixture of American life with the adoption of the Sixteenth Amendment. Many states then began imposing their own income taxes, and municipalities followed suit, with Philadelphia leading off in 1939. By the end of the twentieth century, only New Hampshire and Florida still have no income tax.

69.

1913—B'NAI B'RITH
ANTI-DEFAMATION LEAGUE

The American Jewish service organization B'nai B'rith had originally been founded in 1843. Long associated with orphanage and hospital work and disaster relief, B'nai B'rith took on a new significance in 1913 when it created the Anti-Defamation League. From the start, the league fought discrimination and outright anti-Semitic propaganda. It has been involved in numerous important court cases throughout the century as it worked to establish full respect and civil rights for the American Jewish community.

70.

1913—THE *RITE OF SPRING*

Igor Stravinsky had made a name for himself in 1910 and 1911 with his scores for *The Firebird* and *Petrouchka,* written for Serge Diaghilev's Ballets Russes. Although these strikingly original compositions had distressed the old guard, the premiere of the ballet *Rite of Spring* in 1913 caused a riot in Paris. This was in part due to Stravinsky's score, which made even more daring use of irregular rhythms and harsh dissonance than ever before, but the reaction also stemmed in part from the fact that a peasant fertility rite was being depicted. Once the dust had settled, the ballet went on to become one of the standard works of the repertoire, along with two earlier scores, both for ballet companies and symphony orchestras.

71.

1913—IRISH HOME RULE DEFEATED

A bill granting home rule to Ireland passed the British House of Commons in early January 1913, but was defeated by the House of Lords on January 30. This failure to pass the upper house set the stage for eighty-five years of unrest and bloodshed in Ireland. The Easter Rebellion of 1916, an unsuccessful attempt to establish home rule, was followed by the formation of the Irish Republican Army (IRA) under the leadership of Michael Collins. Its political wing, called the Sinn Fein party, originally founded in 1905, was outlawed by the British government in 1918, but continued to operate underground. Continued violence led to the partition of Ireland, with largely Protestant Northern Ireland being formed in 1920 and the predominantly Catholic Irish Free State formally recognized in 1922. Sinn Fein and the militants of the IRA refused to recognize the partition. The Irish Free State became the sovereign state of Eire under Eamon de Valera in 1937, but remained within the British Commonwealth. During World War II, Eire was officially neutral, and its ports were closed to the British fleet, even though many Irish citizens voluntarily served in the British armed forces. In 1949, total independence was achieved, and the Republic of Ireland withdrew from Commonwealth status. The problems in Northern Ireland, still under British rule, would resurface violently in the 1960s, with a provisional peace plan finally established in 1998 (see entry 363).

72.

1914—SHAKESPEARE AT THE OLD VIC

Lillian Bayliss, ultimately Dame Lillian, founded not only the Old Vic but also the Sadler's Wells Ballet, which would become the Royal Ballet. Her seasons of Shakespeare's plays presented at the Old Victoria Theatre, in an unfashionable part of London across the Thames, began in 1914 and would soon become a mecca for theatergoers and actors. Every great British Shakespearean actor appeared at the Old Vic between 1914 and the late 1970s, when the new National theater complex was built. Laurence Olivier, Edith Evans, John Gielgud, Peggy Ashcroft, Ralph Richardson, Judi Dench—all of whom would eventually be either knighted or made a Dame of the British Empire—became major stars at the Old Vic. So too did many actors who eventually found greater fame in the movies, such as Richard Burton and Anthony Hopkins. For many American visitors to London, the Old Vic was as central an experience as the changing of the guard at Buckingham Palace. No single theater company in the twentieth century had as great an effect as the Old Vic.

73.

1914—ASSASSINATION OF
ARCHDUKE FRANZ FERDINAND

Franz Ferdinand, the heir to the throne of the Austro-Hungarian Empire, was assassinated by a Serbian nationalist at Sarajevo, in what would become Yugoslavia, on June 28, 1914. Europe was already rife with economic and political tensions, and the death of

Archduke Ferdinand would prove the match—or the excuse—that would light the flames of World War I. On one side of the conflict were Germany, Austria-Hungary, and Turkey. On the other were France, Great Britain, and Russia. The United States would finally be drawn into the conflict on the side of France, Great Britain, and Russia in 1917.

74.

1914—THE "ST. LOUIS BLUES"

W.(William) C. (Christopher) Handy (1873–1958) was one of the first to set down jazz music, especially the blues, in the form of song scores. Jazz had developed in the 1890s and would become truly popular in the 1920s, when white musicians began to imitate it. But the true blues were popularized by W. C. Handy as much as anyone else, and his "St. Louis Blues" of 1914 remains one of the most famous and beloved of all blues songs. Handy's influence on other jazz artists and the development of this musical form was profound.

75.

1914—THE ELASTIC BRASSIERE

A New York City designer named Mary Phelps Jacob invented the first elastic brassiere in 1914. It proved much more popular than any previous attempts to provide an alternative to the confining corsets that had been in use for centuries. All modern brassieres are simply further developments of Ms. Jacob's ideas, making use of new materials that have been created throughout the century. Because of the joke involved, many books credit a German named

Titslinger with the invention of the bra, but his was an earlier and far more rigid contraption. Ms. Jacob created the present-day version, lightweight and easily put on or removed. In her way, she was a major contributor to the sexual mores of the century, from the enhancement of feminine beauty to the symbolic "bra burnings" of the 1960s.

76.

1914—THE MACHINE GUN

A descendant of the heavy Gatling gun used at the end of the Civil War, the machine gun steadily improved in design during the first dozen years of the twentieth century. It became lighter and capable of firing more bullets with greater rapidity. During the trench warfare of World War I, it was responsible for millions of deaths on both sides of the conflict. An intensely bloody conflict, but without a single decisive battle, World War I was fought on the same muddy or dusty terrain month after grueling month, year after year. More than ten million soldiers were killed and another twenty million wounded, huge numbers of them victims of machine-gun fire.

77.

1914—BATTLE OF THE MARNE

On September 3, 1914, German forces crossed the river Marne, provoking the first major confrontation of World War I. After a five-day battle between the Germans and the British and French forces, the Germans withdrew but managed to stabilize their lines along the river Aisne. The armies on both sides spent much of the rest of the war dug into trenches, getting nowhere but piling up hundreds of thousands of casualties on both sides. In mid-July, 1918, the Germans once again tried to march toward Paris, but were stopped by the Allied forces. In a sense, both Battles of the Marne, fought nearly four years apart, were stalemates, with nothing but incessant death in between.

78.

1915—TRANSCONTINENTAL PHONE SERVICE

On January 25, 1915, in New York City, Alexander Graham Bell once again spoke the exact words he had in 1876 to his assistant, Dr. Thomas A. Watson: "Mr. Watson, come here, I want you." But in 1876, when Bell made the first successful test of his new invention, the telephone, Watson had been in the next room. Now, after traveling four days by train to the West Coast, he replied to Bell from San Francisco. Thus transcontinental phone service was ceremoniously inaugurated.

79.

1915—"THE METAMORPHOSIS"

One morning Gregor Samsa awoke in his bed to find himself transformed into a gigantic insect." So reads in English translation the opening sentence of Franz Kafka's most famous short story, "The Metamorphosis." A German Jew, born in Prague, Czechoslovakia, Kafka published only short stories and essays during his lifetime, and after he died in 1924 at the age of forty-one, his will instructed his friend and executor Max Brod to burn all his manuscripts. Brod did not do so, seeing to it that the world was given his novels *The Trial*, *The Castle*, and *Amerika*. Kafka's work has proved to be extraordinarily influential, a quintessential example of the twentieth-century concept of "existential dread," which derives from an attempt to make sense on a personal basis of an inexplicable world. Gregor Samsa's endeavor to cope with his new insect existence is one of the strongest of all fictional expressions of this dilemma.

80.

1916—FIRST BIRTH CONTROL CLINIC

Although birth control has been practiced in various ways by cultures around the world from time immemorial, it was not regarded as a subject fit for public discussion until Margaret Higgins Sanger began crusading for it in 1914. When she opened a clinic to dispense birth control advice in Brooklyn in 1916, she was arrested, and she would be incarcerated again and again. By 1925, however, the former nurse had become world famous and organized the first international conference on the subject. Because of religious objections, birth control remains a topic of intense controversy even today, although it has succeeded in keeping population growth from overwhelming the ecosystems of the world.

81.

1916—FIRST WOMAN ELECTED TO
U.S. CONGRESS

Jeannette Rankin, born on a Montana ranch in 1888, became a social worker in Seattle as a young woman, and was soon active in the woman's suffrage movement, working to gain the vote in Washington state, in California, and in her native Montana from 1910 to 1914. Montana gave women the right to vote in 1914, and in 1917 Jeannette Rankin was elected to the United States Congress as Montana's single at-large representative. As the first woman in Congress, she was also its only member to vote against the U.S. Declaration of War with Germany in 1917. A stalwart pacifist, she also voted against the Declaration of War with Japan following Pearl Harbor. Many women members of the House of Representatives, as well as those elected to the Senate, have since shown an independent streak, but none could match Jeannette Rankin in that regard.

82.

1916—EINSTEIN'S GENERAL THEORY
OF RELATIVITY

Among its many other mathematical beauties, Albert Einstein's 1916 development of his 1905 theory of relativity gave an answer to the ancient riddle of whether or not the universe had an edge. By showing that matter warps space, it became clear that the galaxies would wrap around one another to form a sphere, so that if you were able to travel fast enough you would return to your starting point. Einstein's theory stood up to an empirical test in 1919, when the distortion he had predicted in the position of the stars was observed during a solar eclipse. When asked what he would have said if the test had failed, Einstein replied, "I would have had to pity our dear Lord. The theory is correct." It has withstood every test since and become the basis of numerous other discoveries and theories about the nature of the universe.

83.

1916—WILSON NARROWLY WINS REELECTION

President Woodrow Wilson ran for a second term under the slogan He Kept Us Out of War, but even his success in keeping the war in Europe at arm's length did not make him a sure thing. His Republican opponent was the former governor of New York, Charles Evans Hughes, who had stepped down from his position as an associate justice of the United States Supreme Court to run against Wilson. On election night, Hughes went to bed thinking he had won. When a telegram was delivered in the middle of the night, an aide told the Western Union boy that "the President" could not be disturbed, to which the boy replied, "Well, tell the President that he's not President any more." California had finally gone for Wilson, who won with 277 electoral votes to Hughes's 254. Hughes later served as secretary of state under Presidents Harding and Coolidge, then was named Chief Justice of the United States by President Herbert Hoover in 1930, succeeding William Howard Taft in the job and serving until 1941. In 1998, a panel of historians cited Hughes as second only to the great nineteenth-century states-man Henry Clay as the most distinguished candidate for the U.S. presidency to lose the race.

84.

1916—THE BATTLE OF THE SOMME

Perhaps the bloodiest conflict in history to such little effect, the Battle of the Somme took place on the western front in France November 1–19. Historically significant because it was the first bat-tle in which tanks were used, ushering in a new kind of modern warfare, it is remembered most for its terrifying casualty count. The British forces had twenty thousand dead and forty thousand wounded on the first day alone. The total dead and wounded for the British and French over the nineteen days of the battle amounted to 620,000, while the German casualties were 450,000. In the end, the British and French forces had pushed forward about five miles.

85.

1916—LOUIS BRANDEIS NAMED TO
THE SUPREME COURT

In 1916, President Woodrow Wilson broke with the past to name the first Jew, Louis Brandeis, to the United States Supreme Court. As a lawyer, Brandeis had previously revolutionized legal practice by introducing economic and social facts to his argument before the Supreme Court in the 1908 case *Muller* v. *Oregon*. A liberal and a brilliant legal writer, he served as an associate justice of the Supreme Court from 1916 to 1939. Ever since his appointment, U.S. presidents have honored the new tradition of having a "Jewish seat" on the Court.

86.

1916—CLARENCE BIRDSEYE'S
FROZEN FOOD EXPERIMENTS

With his wife and son, Clarence Birdseye went to Labrador on a wildlife expedition in 1916. While there, with few fresh provisions, he began experimenting with the preservation of vegetables and meat by freezing them. Eight years later Birdseye founded his commercial frozen food company, which subsequently became a part of General Foods. He continued his experiments throughout his life, and by 1949 had succeeded in lowering the freezing time required from eighteen hours to a more efficacious hour and a half. By the time of his death in 1956, his revolutionary ideas had given rise to an entirely new way of living in the advanced countries of the world.

87.

1917—UNITED STATES ENTERS WORLD WAR I

When World War I broke out in Europe in the summer of 1914, the majority of Americans felt that it had little to do with them, and that the war would soon be over, anyway. This isolationist view was firmly held by the leaders of Congress, and President Woodrow Wilson made no attempt to counter the prevailing feeling. The United States declared its neutrality on August 4, 1914. But as the war dragged on, disrupting trade and enveloping the home-country relatives of many American immigrants, some voices were raised suggesting that the United States would have to intervene. A major test of isolationist views in America came with the sinking by German submarines of the British liner *Lusitania,* on May 7, 1915, off the Irish coast. Of the 1,195 lives lost with the *Lusitania,* 128 were U.S. citizens. Even that was not enough to draw the United States into the conflict, and in 1916 Woodrow Wilson ran for reelection on the slogan He Kept Us Out of War. But in 1917, Germany stepped up its attacks on American merchant ships carrying goods to England, and the mood shifted. Wilson proclaimed that the "world must be made safe for democracy," and the United States declared war on Germany on April 6, 1917, turning a European conflict into World War I.

88.

1917—THE DRAFT

On May 18, 1917, six weeks after the United States finally entered World War I, a universal draft went into effect. The start of the draft was called Proclamation Day, a name suggested by the secretary of war, Newton D. Baker, to emphasize the patriotic nature of the event. On Lottery Day, July 20, the names of the first ten thousand conscriptees were ceremonially drawn. A total of 2,702,687 men between the ages of twenty-one and thirty were eventually drafted.

89.

1917—THE RUSSIAN REVOLUTION

The defeat of Russia in its 1904–1905 war with Japan created dissension at all levels of society in Russia itself, and an aborted revolution took place at the end of 1905. Czar Nicholas II initially agreed to the creation of an elected parliament, but it was soon dissolved. The loss of life and the economic hardship brought on by World War I, when the country was decimated by Germany, brought new strength to the revolutionary movement, and the czar was forced to abdicate in March 1917. He and his family were subsequently killed (with the possible exception of his daughter Anastasia, whose purported reappearance years later has been the subject of many books and movies and remains controversial).

As in the French Revolution of 1789, the toppling of the royal family led only to dissension among the leaders of various revolutionary groups. After three years of civil wars and devastation, such relatively moderate leaders as Alexander Kerensky were ousted, and the Bolshevik forces under Vladimir Lenin and Leon Trotsky took charge. Lenin died of natural causes in 1924, and the resulting power struggle between the ideological Trotsky and the more narrowly pragmatic Joseph Stalin concluded with Stalin's ascendance.

Trotsky was expelled from Stalin's Soviet Union in 1929, and was ultimately murdered under mysterious circumstances in Mexico in 1940.

90.

1 9 1 7 — P R A V D A

During the Russian Revolution a newspaper was born. It was called *Pravda*, meaning "truth," but it was in fact the mouthpiece for the Communist party and would remain so until the collapse of the Soviet Union. Another newspaper, *Izvestiya*, was founded the same year. *Izvestiya* was the organ of the state, and carried most news concerning foreign relations, while *Pravda* promoted ideological unity. Although it had been the "people's paper" for more than seventy years, *Pravda's* readership shrank drastically following the end of Communist power in 1991. In 1992, it suspended publication, but then was revived as a party broadsheet. Neither *Pravda* nor *Izvestiya* retained anything like its previous readership or power in the post-Communist years.

91.

1 9 1 7 — T H E   W O R D   ''S U R R E A L I S T''   I S   C O I N E D

After seeing Pablo Picasso's sets for the new ballet *Parade*, the French poet and critic Guillaume Apollinaire called them "surrealist." The word would subsequently be applied to his own work as well as that of an entire school of writers and artists influenced by Freud; their work was dedicated to expressing consciousness as experienced in dreams. Picasso, ironically, was never a true member of this movement, whose most famous practitioners were the painters René Magritte and Salvador Dalí. Magritte was a quiet, private man, but the flamboyant Dalí was second only to Picasso as the best self-promoter of the visual artists who came to prominence in the first half of the century. Few paintings have ever become more famous than Dalí's "Persistence of Memory" with its melting watches, and perhaps no other work of art so completely captures the idea of surrealism.

The surrealist movement, officially founded in 1924 with the publication of a Manifesto of Surrealism by André Breton, remained a major influence through the 1930s. Subsequently, its motifs were so completely subsumed into our culture that they are now as likely to appear in an advertisement for automobiles as in a work of art.

92.

1917—TECHNICOLOR MOVIES

The first color film for moving pictures was developed during World War I by Herbert T. Kalmus and Daniel F. Comstock. Initially a two-color system using only red and green, it was first employed in a movie produced in 1917 by Kalmus and Comstock, *The Gulf Between.* An improved version was used for the 1925 silent *The Black Pirate*, starring Douglas Fairbanks, but it remained expensive and unrealistic. In 1932, the two inventors, whose Technicolor company had been incorporated a decade earlier, introduced a three-color process; first used in *Becky Sharp* in 1935. Several of the classic movies of 1939, including *Gone With the Wind* and *The Wizard of Oz*, were in Technicolor, and color movies became increasingly common. However, black-and-white film continued to be widely used for serious dramas. It was not until 1956 that all five movies nominated for Best Picture were in color; the contest was won by

Around the World in 80 Days. Since then there have been only two black-and-white winners, 1960's *The Apartment* and 1993's *Schindler's List,* and the latter used color in its closing sequence.

93.

1917—''READY-MADES'' AS ART

Marcel Duchamp is probably best known to the public for his famous cubist painting "Nude Descending a Staircase," but he was also a major influence on other schools of twentieth-century art. In 1917, he submitted for exhibition a commercially made urinal, to which he applied his signature and gave the title "Fountain." Any visitor to contemporary art exhibitions at major museums and galleries in the 1990s will have viewed many artworks whose nature can be traced directly back to Duchamp's "Fountain." But in 1917, such a work really was "shocking."

94.

1917—THE PULITZER PRIZES

Joseph Pulitzer, born in Hungary in 1847, emigrated to America and became one of its great journalistic figures. With the *New York World,* he became the first to use a tabloid format to attract a mass daily readership. As if to compensate for this venture into "lowest common denominator" journalism, Pulitzer established a large trust fund in his will to found the Columbia School of Journalism and to award annual prizes in journalism and letters. The first awards in 1917, six years after his death, were few in number, but the categories have greatly expanded over the years. There are thirteen prizes in journalism, six in literature and drama as well as a music prize. Panels of judges, which change from year to year, recommend winners in each category, but the final decision is made by the powerful Pulitzer Prize Board, which sometimes overrules the judges. They are the most important such prizes given out in the United States, although there are more recently established awards in specific disciplines that carry larger monetary rewards.

95.

1918—SPANISH FLU EPIDEMIC

The carnage on the battlefields of World War I was echoed around the globe by perhaps the most devastating short-term disease epidemic in the history of the world. What came to be called "Spanish influenza" in fact first appeared at an American military base, Fort Riley, in Kansas, during March 1918. It spread like wild-fire among the American military and then around the world. It would not be until the 1930s that the class of viruses that cause influenza was discovered, and medical authorities were at a loss to contain its spread or treat its symptoms. People either lived or died, and they died at horrifying rates. By late summer, American troop-ships crossing from the United States to the war in Europe lost dozens (and in some cases hundreds) of soldiers to the flu before they even faced German artillery. The civilian population was devastated as well. By the time the flu disappeared as mysteriously as it had arrived, in November, just as the armistice was being signed, 21,640,000 people had died from it, 12.5 million in India alone. The Spanish flu epidemic killed more than 500,000 Americans, and inspired a macabre little rhyme: "I had a little bird and his name was Enza. I opened the door and in flew Enza." On a higher plane, the epidemic inspired one of the greatest American short novels, *Pale Horse, Pale Rider,* by Katharine Anne Porter.

96.

1918—DAYLIGHT SAVING TIME

When daylight saving time begins in April each year, clocks are set forward one hour to provide more usable daylight hours. It was first inaugurated in the United States, Great Britain, Australia, and even Germany, during World War I as a means of conserving power and the raw materials necessary to the production of power. While almost all the states take advantage of daylight saving time, they are not required to do so. That has led to some peculiarities over the decades, with people crossing state lines having to adjust their awareness of time, if not their watches. For example, people living just over the Indiana border from Chicago, and working in that Illinois city, have found themselves dealing with an hour's difference between home and work because of the different daylight saving schedules in the two states.

97.

1918—KNUTE ROCKNE BECOMES COACH AT
NOTRE DAME

Between his installation as Notre Dame football coach in 1918 and 1931, when he was killed in a plane crash, Knute Rockne's teams would win 105 games against 12 losses and 5 ties. When his small but extremely fast backfield players ran over Army in 1924, Grantland Rice wrote: "Outlined against a blue-gray October sky, the four horsemen rode again. In dramatic lore they are known as Famine, Pestilence, Destruction and Death. These are only aliases. Their real names are Stuhldreher, Miller, Crowley and Layden." Rockne also would pass into political history because of the movie

Knute Rockne: All American (1940), in which Pat O'Brien played the title role and Rockne's star player was portrayed by Ronald Reagan. Reagan's line, "win just one for the Gipper" (the Gipper being Rockne), would become a recurrent phrase throughout Reagan's subsequent political career.

98.

1919—THE TREATY OF VERSAILLES

There were several important treaties signed at Versailles, the palace built in the midseventeenth century by Louis XIV, the Sun King. But the most famous, the Treaty of Versailles, was the one agreed to by the United States, France, Great Britain, and Italy that brought an end to World War I and imposed harsh penalties on Germany for its aggression. The treaty was personally negotiated by President Woodrow Wilson of the United States, Prime Minister Lloyd George of Great Britain, Premier Clemenceau of France, and Premier Orlando of Italy. In addition to returning Alsace and Lorraine to France and ceding much of Prussia to Poland, thus undoing the treaties of earlier wars, it also called for the creation of the League of Nations. This was the fruition of President Wilson's vision of an international body that would help to prevent future wars. But isolationists in the United States Senate refused to ratify the League of Nations, giving Wilson a bitter defeat, and sowing the seeds of World War II.

99.

1919—PROHIBITION RATIFIED

The shortest-lived and most ineffective amendment to the United States Constitution was ratified by the required two thirds of the states on January 29, 1919. The Eighteenth Amendment banned "The manufacture, sale or transportation of intoxicating liquors." But it would be nearly a year before Prohibition went into effect. The Volstead Act, passed by the U.S. Congress to put enforcement teeth into the amendment, set the level of liquor so low that even beer and wine were prohibited. President Woodrow Wilson had vetoed the Volstead Act, but the veto had been overridden, and the Act was then challenged in the courts. The U.S. Supreme Court upheld the Volstead Act on January 5, 1920, and Prohibition went into official effect the next day.

Enter the great era of bootlegging, with its violent criminals like Al Capone and its "gentleman" dealers like Joseph P. Kennedy. Speakeasies and bathtub gin proliferated, and law enforcement agencies never had anywhere near the amount of money necessary to enforce the amendment. Police officers were routinely paid off, and many critics began to say that Prohibition was doing far more to damage the moral climate of the nation than drinking ever had. Congress finally threw in the towel and repealed the Eighteenth Amendment, nullifying it with the Twenty-first Amendment on December 5, 1933. Repeal went through with amazing speed, with the necessary thirty-sixth state—Utah, home to the teetotaling Mormons, of all places—ratifying it on April 10, 1934. The most disastrous attempt to legislate private behavior in U.S. history was dead.

100.

1919—FIRST NONSTOP FLIGHT ACROSS ATLANTIC

Competing for a 10,000-pound-sterling prize, aviators John Alcock and Arthur Whitten Brown flew a Vickers Vimy bomber from World War I, a biplane with two Rolls-Royce "Eagle" engines, from Newfoundland to Ireland. Both men had flown for the British in World War I (Brown was an American but had been born in Glasgow, taking British citizenship to do so). When they landed in Ireland, they had been in the air for sixteen hours and twenty-eight minutes, a record that would stand until Charles Lindbergh's solo flight in 1927.

101.

1920—COMMERCIAL RADIO

The first regular radio broadcasts anywhere in the world began in the United States in 1920, providing endless entertainment and bringing the news of the world into the American home faster than before. Radio would make the country more cohesive than it had ever been, and would sow the seeds for the formation of a popular culture that would come to define the country with the advent of television thirty years later. Did these first radio broadcasts start in New York, Chicago, or even Hollywood? No, they were local to East Pittsburgh, Pennsylvania. Within three years, Calvin Coolidge, who had succeeded to the presidency following Warren Harding's sudden death in August 1923, gave the first nationally broadcast speech by a United States president when he addressed Congress on December 5, 1923.

102.

1920—THE PLAGUE IN INDIA

It is commonly thought that bubonic plague, known as the "Black Death" because it left corpses the color of mud, was a scourge of the Middle Ages. In fact, the last great epidemic of bubonic plague occurred in India in 1920, killing at least two million people. Even though it had been known for centuries that the plague was carried by rats, unsanitary conditions in India, and the lack of medical facilities, allowed the disease to wreak its horrors one last dreadful time. Medical knowledge is one thing; the funds and expertise to put it to use are another. Indeed, there are those who warn that even now it is possible to see a new outbreak of bubonic plague in vastly overpopulated and underdeveloped parts of the world.

103.

1920—ROBOTS

The art director of the National Theater of Prague, who also wrote widely on gardening and travel, had a play produced in 1920 that quickly became a huge success around the world. The author's name was Karel Capek, and his play was called *R.U.R.* These letters stood for "Rossum's Universal Robots," soulless, manufactured creatures with expressionless humanoid faces. The word "robot" was derived from a Slavic root for "work." The concept of automatons who would do the dirty work for humans became a fundamental theme of twentieth-century science fiction, and the word "robot" entered the language. Capek's creatures were biological in nature (today they would be called androids or even clones); by the 1930s, the word "robot" was reserved for machinelike creatures made of metal. It should be noted that Capek's robots turned on their masters and destroyed civilization—another theme that has been endlessly played out in fictional scenarios.

104.

1920—HERCULE POIROT MAKES HIS ENTRANCE

The year 1920 saw the publication of such major works of literature as Colette's *Cheri*, *Main Street* by Sinclair Lewis, and *The Age of Innocence* by Edith Wharton. But for the average reader, the most important literary event of the year was undoubtedly Agatha

Christie's introduction of a new character, Hercule Poirot, in *The Mysterious Affair at Styles*. The cunning but fussy Belgian private detective, a resident of England, became so popular that Mrs. Christie, thoroughly sick of him, was strongly tempted to kill him off, as Arthur Conan Doyle had with Sherlock Holmes. Instead she introduced other characters, like Miss Marple in 1930, and continued to return to Poirot's exploits at intervals right up until her death in 1976.

105.

1920—WOMEN GET THE VOTE

Sensible and responsible women do not want to vote. The relative positions assumed by man and woman in the working out of our civilization were assigned long ago by a higher intelligence than ours." So said former President Grover Cleveland in 1905. The fact that he felt the need to speak out suggests that the women's suffrage movement, which had begun at a Seneca Falls, New York, convention in 1848, was finally getting someplace. In 1878, in fact, a constitutional amendment had been introduced in the United States Congress by Senator Aaron A. Sargent. It read: "The right of citizens of the United States to vote shall not be denied or abridged by the United States or by any states on account of sex." For the next forty-two years this amendment, with the same wording, was introduced in every new Congress. Finally, on August 18, 1920, the youngest member of Congress, twenty-four-year-old Harry Burn, cast the last vote for passage, saying, "Hurrah! And vote for suffrage!" It turned out that his mother had told him to vote for the amendment or else! President Woodrow Wilson declared the amendment ratified by proclamation on August 26, and a sixty-two-year-long struggle was finally over.

Similar struggles had taken place in other countries, with suffragettes in Great Britain interrupting parliamentary debate, chaining themselves to fences, and instituting strikes. Women over thirty who met certain educational and property requirements had gained the vote in Great Britain in 1918, but the right for all women over twenty-one to vote did not come until 1928. This delay had occurred in part because so many British men had died in World War I that women would otherwise have been the majority among voters.

106.

1920—MISS AMERICA

On September 7, 1920, Atlantic City, New Jersey, was host to the first Miss America contest. The most famous beauty pageant in the world has been held in Atlantic City ever since. The rules have changed over the years to reflect changing mores and views of women, but when television viewers were asked to vote in 1997 whether the bathing suit competition should be discontinued, they gave it a strong vote of confidence. The contestants are better educated than they once were, and the talent competition has become increasingly professional, but the main attraction remains the display of wholesome, pretty American women from big cities and small towns across the nation.

107.

1920—WARREN G. HARDING ELECTED PRESIDENT

Warren G. Harding was a Republican senator from Ohio, and one of the least able men ever elected president. He was chosen at a fractious convention as a compromise; party leaders thought that they could control him, and that his silver-haired handsomeness would appeal to women voters, who would be casting their first votes for president. His Democratic opponent, James M. Cox of Ohio, was also a compromise candidate and nearly as undistinguished. Harding won a huge victory, 404 electoral votes to 127 for Cox. When he died suddenly in 1923, the full scope of the scandals surrounding him was not yet known, and he was deeply mourned. But not only did he preside over a deeply corrupt administration, he knew he was not up to the job and had tearfully admitted as much to friends.

108.

1920—LEAGUE OF WOMEN VOTERS

The National American Woman Suffrage Association had led the fight to gain the vote for women since the nineteenth century, but when the Nineteenth Amendment was adopted in 1920, the movement split argumentatively into two parts. One group continued to press for an equal rights amendment for women and to take strong feminist views on many other subjects. A more moderate segment founded the League of Women Voters. The league's first aim was to educate women about the rights and responsibilities of voting. Later, it took on the broader task of improving the political process in general. Strictly nonpartisan, the league has sponsored the televised presidential debates since they began in 1960.

109.

1920—100 MILLION STRONG

The 1920 census revealed that there were 105,710,620 Americans and that for the first time the majority of them lived in cities. The United States had become an industrial giant; Presidents Theodore Roosevelt and Woodrow Wilson had both won the Nobel Peace Prize, Roosevelt in 1906 for settling the Russo-Japanese War, and Wilson in 1920 for his vision of a more peaceful world as embodied in the League of Nations; and women had the vote. It was already clear that this was likely to be "the American Century." The only sour note was the refusal of the United States Congress, once again controlled by isolationists, to approve U.S. participation in the League of Nations. That refusal would pave the way for Hitler's rise, and America would once again have to come to Europe's rescue.

110.

1921—KU KLUX KLAN RESURFACES

The original Ku Klux Klan had been founded in 1866 by the former Confederate general Nathan Bedford Forrest and others to oppose Reconstruction policies following the Civil War. Various states, beginning with Tennessee, soon passed laws against its extralegal activities of intimidation, which were used as much against whites as blacks, and the Klan was officially defunct by 1869. But a new and more militant Klan, founded in 1915, began making headlines in 1921 with major rallies at which virulent anti-Catholic and anti-Semitic sentiments were expressed. By the end of the 1920s, it had once again gone underground, but had a new upsurge during the 1960s, when it violently opposed civil rights activities, murdering both blacks and the white civil rights workers who went south to help them. While the Klan has usually been depicted in novels and movies in terms of lynchings of blacks, its broader nativist beliefs were of equal concern. It was more than a white supremacist organization in all its incarnations, in that it espoused opposition to all those who were "different" because of racial or religious background. Those nativist ideas are very much to the forefront in today's attenuated Klan activities.

111.

1921—GERMANY GIVEN $132 BILLION
REPARATIONS BILL

On April 27, 1921, the German government was presented with a final demand for $132 billion in reparation payments to the Allied countries that had defeated Germany in World War I. This staggering amount, punitive in the extreme, would cripple the German economy and lead to soaring inflation. The economic situation in Germany became so bad that in the late 1920s it took a wheelbarrow full of paper money to buy a day's worth of groceries. In the view of most historians, the reparations requirements sowed the seeds of anger that would permit the rise of Hitler over the next dozen years.

112.

1921—TOMB OF THE UNKNOWN SOLDIER

Originally called the "Unknown Warrior," the body of an unidentified American soldier was interred at Arlington National Cemetery on November 15, 1921. This tribute to those who gave their lives in World War I was, *The New York Times* wrote, like no ceremony ever before witnessed in Washington, D.C.: "Surrounded by the world's great, with none of them too great to bow in homage, this dead boy's funeral was still no pageant [but] more a benediction . . ."

There would be further memorials to unknown soldiers at the end of World War II, the Korean War, and the Vietnam War. In 1998, the Vietnam "unknown" was removed from the grave, identified by DNA analysis, and the body returned to the family. Because DNA testing makes it possible to establish individual identity from minute samples of human tissue, it seemed unlikely that future wars would result in unknown remains, and that the tradition of having a tomb of an unknown warrior was at an end.

113.

1921—THE PERFUME OF THE CENTURY

On May 5, 1921, the French designer Coco Chanel introduced a new perfume that she called Chanel No. 5. Coco Chanel had already demonstrated an instinct for the classic line in women's suits, which would remain in style with amazingly minor modifications for much of the century, but she topped herself with this perfume, which is still going strong almost eighty years later. There have been thousands of other scents put on the market, many of them all the rage for a while, and in the last few decades "celebrity" perfumes have become very popular, most recently those of Elizabeth Taylor. But nothing has matched the staying power of Chanel No. 5.

114.

1922 — READER'S DIGEST

DeWitt Wallace and his wife, Lila Acheson, published the first issue of *Reader's Digest* in 1922. The monthly magazine, with its selection of short articles from other publications, condensed versions of best-selling books, human-interest stories, jokes, and cartoons, would become one of the greatest magazine publishing successes in the world. It long held the title of the largest-circulation magazine, with more than seventeen million readers, but was ultimately overtaken by *TV Guide* in the 1980s. Widely disparaged by the literary world, especially for its condensed books, the magazine's first issue was published in—of all places—Greenwich Village in New York City, then the hotbed of avant-garde writing, but it soon moved to Chicago.

115.

1922 — ABIE'S IRISH ROSE

This comedy about the romance between a Jewish boy and an Irish lass opened on Broadway in June 1922 to some of the worst reviews in the history of the American theater. One of its most prominent detractors was Robert Benchley, then the critic of *Life* magazine and later of *The New Yorker*. One of the famed wits of the Algonquin Round Table, Benchley also wrote and starred in a series of hilarious Hollywood short subjects in the 1930s, winning an Academy Award for 1935's *How to Sleep*. He wrote of *Abie's Irish Rose*, "Something awful." A year later he was still trying to steer people away from it: "America's favorite comedy. God forbid." The play ran for five years and five months. It is still regarded by theater historians as the worst hit play in Broadway history. But that just proves one of the great truths of theater criticism. Critics can close down a serious play overnight, but there is nothing they can do to prevent the public from flocking to popular entertainment that gets good word of mouth. *Abie's Irish Rose* is a primary example of why hope springs eternal among Broadway producers.

116.

1922—*THE WASTE LAND*

Thomas Stearns Eliot was born in St. Louis, Missouri, and attended Harvard University, but starting in his mid-twenties, in 1914, he moved to England and became a British subject in 1927. One of the most influential poets of the century, his longest and most complex work of poetry (he also wrote notable plays and essays) was *The Waste Land,* published in 1922 to immediate acclaim. While its subject was the anguish and barrenness of modern life, and although it contained an enormous number of literary, religious, and historical references, many simply hinted at in a word or two, the surface beauty and vividness of the verse made it appealing to many who grasped only a few of its layered meanings. It is regarded as one of the greatest and most central literary works of the century. T. S. Eliot was awarded the Nobel Prize in Literature in 1948. He also won a Broadway Tony Award in 1983, eighteen years after his death, for his lyrics to the musical *Cats,* which were drawn from a book of light verse and set to music by composer Anthony Lloyd Webber. He had also won a Tony for Best Play for his enigmatic *The Cocktail Party* in 1950. But it is *The Waste Land* that remains his masterpiece.

117.

1923—TUT-ANKH-AMEN'S INNER TOMB OPENED

In Luxor, Egypt, on February 16, 1923, the inner tomb of the grave of King Tut-Ankh-Amen was opened, revealing treasures of such magnificence that they put all previous discoveries of Egyptian antiquities to shame. Most tombs of the ancient Egyptian kings had been plundered over the centuries, and their contents scattered or even melted down for the gold of which they were made. King Tut's undisturbed tomb, discovered in 1922 by Howard Carter and the earl of Carnarvon, would not only reveal dazzling treasures of unparalleled beauty, but greatly advance the study of ancient Egypt. Because King Tut, who had lived circa 1350 B.C., had surrounded himself with a virtual catalog of the artifacts of his time, historians, archeologists, and linguists were able to put the king's ancient world in an entirely new perspective. The beauty of the artifacts has enthralled the world ever since, and the popular imagination was stirred by this discovery more than any other in any century. This was in no small part due to Howard Carter's account of his epic discovery, which even today can be read with a sense of breathless excitement akin to that brought on by the Indiana Jones movies of a half-century later.

118.

1923—EARTHQUAKE IN JAPAN KILLS 500,000

On September 1, 1923, a massive earthquake devastated hundreds of cities and towns in Japan, virtually destroying Yokohama and Tokyo, as a result of buildings having been either flattened by the quake or burned by the fires that followed. Three other cities were hit almost as hard and millions of people were left homeless. Like the San Francisco earthquake of 1906, which killed only a thousand but brought fires that destroyed most of the city, the Japanese earthquake of 1923 fostered great changes in architecture and building codes that were subsequently adopted in earthquake zones around the world.

119.

1923—SOUND PICTURES

Thomas Edison had pioneered the use of sound with motion pictures, but because the sound was provided by a phonograph record, and all too liable to get out of sync with the picture, it saw limited use. Iowa-born Lee De Forest was the first to develop a process that imprinted the sound track directly on to the film itself. However, Hollywood studios were initially resistant to De Forest's invention. Not only would the cost of movies increase with his process, but many of the major silent-movie stars had voices that the studios knew would not be acceptable to the public. When Al Jolson's *The Jazz Singer* was released in July 1928, though, the public went wild, and all the major studios rushed sound pictures into production. Like many inventors before and after, De Forest was squeezed out by major corporations, and never received either the credit or financial reward he deserved.

120.

1923—THE CHARLESTON

The dance that was to become emblematic of the 1920s and the Jazz Age was first introduced in the Ziegfeld Follies, playing at New York's Amsterdam Theater, in 1922. Jazz had been banned from Broadway two years earlier as an affront to morality, and showman Flo Ziegfeld was pushing the limits by introducing this jazz-influenced dance. Within a year, the Charleston had become the rage of the New York dance halls and quickly spread across the country. Many older people found it shocking, but they were shocked by the short hair and skirts young women were wearing, too.

121.

1924—THE FIRST WINTER OLYMPICS

The modern Olympic Games had begun in Athens, Greece, in 1896, and were celebrated each four years after that in different locales. The Games had been interrupted by World War I, but were resumed in 1920. These were what we now call the Summer Olympic Games, devoted to track-and-field events. In 1924, however, the first Winter Olympic Games were held in Chamonix, France. Ironically, part of the impetus for the creation of a Winter Games had come from the fact that figure skating had been included in the track-and-field events in 1908 in London, England, and in 1920 in Antwerp, Belgium, making use of newly built indoor rinks. The alpine and northern European countries that specialized in skiing events demanded that a Winter Games be created that would give them a chance to compete along with figure skaters. Thus figure skating, which some critics have claimed is not a sport (a claim hotly contested by anyone who can do a triple revolution jump), played a central role in the creation of the Winter Olympics.

122.

1924—J. EDGAR HOOVER

In 1924, J. Edgar Hoover was appointed acting director of what was then called the Bureau of Investigation. He would soon get the job for keeps—and then some, serving for forty-eight years as director of an agency he completely transformed. The renamed Federal Bureau of Investigation, or FBI, became widely popular in the 1930s for its pursuit of such criminals as John Dillinger, and its ''Ten Most Wanted'' list entered into national folklore. Hoover was slow even to admit the existence of the Mafia, but moved against it with considerable effect in later decades. The FBI became more controversial from the mid-1950s on, tainted to some degree by the excesses of McCarthyism and by its own obsession with left-wingers. There were often rumblings that each new president would get rid of J. Edgar Hoover, but as he continued to head the organization well into his seventies, it began to be suggested that no one dared fire him because he had so much dirt on them in his files. He finally retired in 1972 at the age of seventy-seven, and died in 1975. After his death, it came out that he was homosexual and had even enjoyed dressing in drag, adding an entirely new perspective to the story of America's most famous crimebuster of the century.

123.

1924—WEISSMULLER SETS WORLD RECORD

At the 1924 Olympic Games, handsome Johnny Weissmuller of the United States set a world record in the 100-meter freestyle swimming event, one of sixty-seven records he would set between 1921 and 1929, when, at the age of twenty-four, he stopped swimming competitively. At those 1924 Games, he also won two other gold medals, in the 400-meter freestyle and as the anchor of 800-meter freestyle relay. Weissmuller was responsible for turning swimming into a "glamour" sport in the United States. He is probably even better remembered today because of his second career in movies, in which he played Tarzan in a dozen films, starting in 1932.

124.

1924—CALVIN COOLIDGE ELECTED
IN HIS OWN RIGHT

Calvin Coolidge had gained a national reputation when, as governor of Massachusetts, he had put down the Boston police strike in 1919, and he was untouched by such Harding administration scandals as Teapot Dome, having been completely on the sidelines as vice president. When he succeeded to the presidency on Harding's death, he proved to be a steady hand, and he was easily elected in his own right in 1924, beating John W. Davis of New York by 382 electoral votes to 136. Davis had been chosen on the 103rd ballot at an almost riotous Democratic convention, a "compromise" candidate if ever there was one.

125.

1924—NATIVE AMERICANS GIVEN CITIZENSHIP

Many Native American tribes were initially friendly to European settlers on the American continent. The Pilgrims gave credit to Samoset of the Permaquid tribe and Squanto of the Pawtuxet tribe for their very survival during the first two winters at Plymouth Colony. But the European immigrants, including the Puritan descendants of the Pilgrims, began to push Indian tribes out of their ancestral lands well before the start of the eighteenth century. By the nineteenth century, bloody conflicts between Americans and the native tribes were almost constant. During the years 1853–1856, fifty-two treaties were signed with Indian tribes, but the United States government eventually broke every one of them.

In the early twentieth century, a movement arose to treat Native Americans more fairly. While most of them lived on the reservations they had been shunted off to, conditions *did* improve, and in 1924 they were accorded citizenship in the land they had once ruled. Most states granted them the right to vote, but Arizona did not do so until 1948, nor did Maine until 1954 or New Mexico until 1962. In all three cases, the move was forced by federal court decree. The famous 1924 photograph of President Calvin Coolidge in an Indian headdress was occasioned by the granting of citizenship to Native Americans. By 1929, the United States had a vice president, Charles Curtis of Kansas, who had Native American heritage, being part Kaw. That is the highest office held to date by a person with a Native American heritage, although there have been U.S. representatives, senators, and state governors of Indian ancestry.

126.

1924 — BILLY BUDD

Herman Melville, after years at sea, had considerable commercial and literary success with novels such as *Typee* (1846) and *Omoo* (1847), but his massive novel *Moby-Dick* (1851) was not well received, and *Pierre* (1852) was widely scorned. Melville continued to write short novels, but they, too, were largely ignored, and he was so discouraged that he put his final work, *Billy Budd*, written three years before his 1891 death, in a trunk. He was almost entirely forgotten by the 1920s, when *Moby-Dick* was republished and recognized as perhaps the greatest of all American novels. The publication of the newly discovered *Billy Budd* in 1924 cemented his newfound reputation. That late masterpiece later became the basis for an opera of the same name by the British composer Benjamin

Britten that has become part of the repertory of opera houses around the world. Every century produces great artists who are not understood in their own time. The restoration of Herman Melville's reputation is widely regarded as one of the most important examples of belated artistic approval to have occurred in the twentieth century.

127.

1925—SCOTCH TAPE INVENTED

The invention of what sometimes seems like a primary way of holding civilization together occurred in 1925. But it came into being not for the reasons that one might expect. Detroit car manufacturers were just beginning to get fancy in the use of colored paint on automobiles, and were having problems achieving a sharp distinction between two different colors. They asked the 3M Company of Minnesota to come up with a solution, and Scotch tape was born. Like Kleenex, Scotch tape is a brand name that has entered the language as a general term, and appears on people's shopping lists no matter what brand they may actually end up buying.

128.

1925—THE ''MONKEY TRIAL''

Charles Darwin's theory of evolution had been published in *Origin of Species* in 1859. Over the ensuing decades, it had been universally accepted by scientists as well as by most of the educated public. But in the Bible Belt of the American South it was still regarded by many as heresy in the 1920s. Tennessee had passed a law making it illegal to teach Darwinian theory in schools, and when a young teacher named John T. Scopes taught evolution anyway, he was brought to trial in July 1925. America's foremost lawyer, Clarence Darrow, arrived to defend him. The prosecution was advised by William Jennings Bryan, who had three times been the unsuccessful Democratic candidate for president, in 1896, 1900, and 1908.

There have been many so-called trials of the century, including that of Sacco and Vanzetti, the Lindbergh kidnapping trial, and the O. J. Simpson trial at the century's close. In terms of intellectual content (and its reverse), the Scopes trial certainly prevails. Despite all the evidence of science that was marshaled and all of Darrow's eloquence, the jury found Scopes guilty, although he was subsequently released because of a technicality. Tennessee did not repeal the law forbidding the teaching of evolution until 1967, and to this day there are many fundamentalist Christians who seek to have Darwin's ideas outlawed.

129.

1925—*THE NEW YORKER* FOUNDED

In 1925, Harold Ross founded a new magazine called *The New Yorker*, which would soon become America's most widely read periodical of its kind, publishing fiction and essays by many of the country's finest writers, together with sophisticated cartoons, reviews of the arts, and cultural chatter. Famous for its satirical covers and its major works of nonfiction like John Hersey's *Hiroshima*, James Baldwin's *The Fire Next Time*, and Truman Capote's *In Cold Blood*, it nevertheless began to lose readers and money in the 1980s. With changes under the editorship of Tina Brown in the 1990s, it regained its status and may yet become profitable again. No matter its eventual fate, it published more fiction and essays of importance than any other American magazine during the twentieth century.

130.

1925—GEORGE BERNARD SHAW WINS
THE NOBEL PRIZE

The Nobel Prize for Literature has generated more controversy than any other Nobel category, even the Peace Prize. The prize was not given to Henry James (whose last and greatest novels were written in the twentieth century), or to James Joyce or Marcel Proust, whose works are cornerstones of modern literature. It did go to the three greatest playwrights of the century, all of whom happened to be of Irish descent: George Bernard Shaw, Eugene O'Neill, and Samuel Beckett. O'Neill was as American as he was Irish, and Beckett spent most of his adult life in Paris, wrote his plays in French, and then translated them into English. It could be said that Shaw was in some ways as English as he was Irish, and his plays were often more "commercial," and popular, than those of O'Neill and Beckett. From satirical comedies like the early *Arms and the Man* (1894), *Major Barbara* (1905), and the ever-popular basis for *My Fair Lady, Pygmalion* (1913), to the very serious *St. Joan*, and the great *Heartbreak House* (1919), Shaw's works showed an enormous breadth of subject and style. None of his works, some critics feel, approach the depth of feeling in O'Neill's *A Long Day's Journey into Night* (first produced posthumously in 1955) or the originality and universality of Beckett's *Waiting for Godot* (1953), but critics express little doubt that Shaw, O'Neill, and Beckett will be long regarded as among the century's most brilliant writers.

131.

1925 — COUNTRY MUSIC GAINS POPULARITY

Country music began to gain in popularity outside its epicenter in Tennessee during 1925. This was due to two new radio programs. One, *Family Music from Nashville,* was a variety program, and the other made direct broadcasts from the Grand Ole Opry in Nashville. The first programs went on the air November 28, and the second on December 10. Country music continued to draw new devotees for the rest of the century, finally finding avid fans in the big cities on both coasts in the 1980s and 1990s.

132.

1926—THE EIGHT-HOUR DAY

As more and more workers sought to unionize in the 1920s, Henry Ford tried to keep that eventuality at bay by having his company adopt an eight-hour day and a five-day week. For a while, this tactic worked, but in 1937 major strikes against the Detroit car manufacturers finally led to the recognition of the United Automobile Workers. Nevertheless, Ford's company was the first major American manufacturer to adopt the eight-hour day, and its example caused many other companies to follow suit. In some cases, other companies copied Ford's tactic as a way of staving off unionization. Still others adopted the eight-hour day because it proved to be a sound business practice, and during the 1930s it gradually became standard throughout U.S. business and industry.

133.

1926—GERTRUDE EDERLE SWIMS THE ENGLISH CHANNEL

The waters of the English Channel were so rough on August 6, 1926, that steamship crossings were canceled that day. This didn't stop nineteen-year-old American swimmer Gertrude ("Trudy") Ederle from smearing herself with grease and making her planned attempt to become the first woman to swim across the Channel. Five men had done it before her—and hundreds had failed. Trudy not only became the first woman to swim the Channel, but surpassed the time of her male predecessors. Although her hearing was permanently affected by the pounding she took that day in the roiling waters, she was fully able to register the cheers of nearly a million people who thronged the streets of New York for the ticker-tape parade that she was accorded on her return to America.

134.

1926—BOOK-OF-THE-MONTH CLUB FOUNDED

There had long been best-seller lists to alert the American public to what was popular reading, but the founding of the Book-of-the-Month Club in 1926 marked a new way of getting people to read not only best-sellers, but also worthwhile books that they might otherwise overlook. The books offered through the mail by the club were chosen by a distinguished board of literary judges, whose job it was both to cater to public preferences and to expand the scope of those preferences at the same time. The success of the club was disparaged by some academicians as solidifying "middle-brow" tastes, but in fact the selections managed to be fairly daring at times, and the club has generally been credited with raising the horizons of millions of readers. The club's format, with a catalog of offerings each month, and the necessity of returning a reply card if the main selection wasn't wanted, has been copied to the point of becoming ubiquitous in the marketing of cultural artifacts, and has been adapted by scores of companies as a way to sell everything from fruit to nuts.

135.

1926—THE DEATH OF VALENTINO

The Italian-born American silent-screen star Rudolph Valentino became a sensation in 1921's *The Four Horsemen of the Apocalypse*. In the same year, he made *The Sheik*, which brought him the adoration of American women, and his films over the next several years only increased the level of devotion of his female fans. Many men were somewhat skeptical about this heavily made-up romantic hero, but that seemed only to make him more popular with women. When he died in 1926 at the age of thirty-one of acute appendicitis, women all over the country wept and fainted. His New York funeral turned into a virtual riot scene. Valentino was the first creation of Hollywood to engender such passionate responses, foreshadowing the effect on the public of the premature deaths of later stars like Marilyn Monroe, James Dean, and Elvis Presley. Their cults are still with us, since they died in the second half of the century, but Valentino was the first movie star whose death brought on virtual hysteria, and accounts from that time suggest that the emotional reaction was even greater than was the case with the later legends.

136.

1926—LIQUID FUEL ROCKET

In 1920, *The New York Times* published an editorial ridiculing a young scientist named Robert H. Goddard, a professor at Clark University in Massachusetts, who the previous year had written a scientific paper about the means of sending rockets to the moon. Goddard persisted in his work, despite widespread criticism even by other scientists, and in 1926 launched the first liquid fuel rocket from his own backyard. Ten years later, when Goddard was launching experimental rockets in New Mexico, the Nazi government sent a spy to report on his work. His ideas continued to be ignored in the United States, but the Germans drew on them in the development of the V-2 rockets used against Britain in World War II. After the war, as German rocket scientists like Wernher von Braun came to the United States, Goddard's pioneering efforts began to be properly recognized, and the Goddard Space Center was named after him. A month before *Apollo 11* landed on the moon, on July 20, 1969, *The New York Times* formally retracted its 1920 editorial lambasting Goddard.

137.

1926—"POOH"

The year 1926 saw the publication of Ernest Hemingway's first novel, *The Sun Also Rises,* Franz Kafka's posthumous *The Castle,* and T. E. Lawrence's account of his exploits in Arabia, *The Seven Pillars of Wisdom,* but there are those who would say, "Pooh to all that," for 1926 also brought into the world A. A. Milne's *Winnie the Pooh.* This beguiling account of Christopher Robin and his adventures with his teddy bear, Winnie the Pooh, and other denizens of Pooh Corner, like Eeyore the donkey and Roo, the baby kangaroo, would join such classics as L. Frank Baum's *The Wonderful Wizard of Oz* and Kenneth Grahame's *The Wind in the Willows* among the most-loved books of the century. Lest anyone suggest that Pooh is not to be taken seriously, an international campaign was launched in 1998 to try to get the original stuffed bear that belonged to Milne's son returned to England from America, where it resides in the collection of the New York Public Library at the Donnell Branch opposite the Museum of Modern Art.

138.

1927—LINDBERGH'S SOLO ATLANTIC FLIGHT

On May 20, 1927, twenty-five-year-old Charles Augustus Lindbergh took off from Roosevelt Field on Long Island in an attempt to make the first nonstop solo flight across the Atlantic Ocean. Prize money had been offered to the first aviator to succeed at such a flight, but no one had come close to success, and few thought Lindbergh would make it either. As his plane, the *Spirit of St. Louis,* was spotted off the French coast, thousands of people rushed to Le Bourget airport, most in the expectation of seeing him crash. But he had correctly calculated how much fuel he would need for his 33-hour, 29½-minute flight of 3,610 miles, and landed smoothly. The crowds who had come to witness a disaster erupted in pandemonium, having seen instead the beginning of a new age. For some time to come, Charles Lindbergh would be the most famous human being on the planet.

139.

1927—CAR INSURANCE

With automobiles rolling off the Detroit assembly lines by the millions, road accidents were becoming increasingly common. Henry Ford's wish to see a car in every garage was on its way to becoming a reality, but this also meant that sooner or later there would be a dent in every fender, at the least. Massachusetts became the first state, in 1927, to make car insurance mandatory. This idea spread rapidly across the country, and almost as rapidly gave rise to outcries that the insurance rates were too high—a complaint that can threaten the reelection of politicians to this day.

140.

1927—EXECUTION OF SACCO AND VANZETTI

On August 22, 1927, Nicola Sacco and Bartolelmeo Vanzetti were executed in Massachusetts after years of appeals for the 1920 murder of a paymaster and his guard in Braintree, Massachusetts. Both men were anarchists, and it was widely believed that they had been convicted more for their political beliefs than on the basis of the flimsy evidence against them. Like the Dreyfus case in France in the 1890s, in which Captain Alfred Dreyfus, a Jew, was convicted of treason, the Sacco-Vanzetti case became a worldwide cause, and arguments about their guilt or innocence continued for decades. Governor Michael Dukakis of Massachusetts, who would become the Democratic nomineee for president in 1988, granted Sacco and Vanzetti posthumous pardons in 1977 during his first year as governor of Massachusetts.

141.

1927—BABE RUTH SETS HOME-RUN RECORD

The most famous player in the history of baseball, George Herman ("Babe") Ruth became a major league pitcher with the Boston Red Sox, winning eighty-seven games and losing only forty-four in the years 1914–1919. He was such a powerful hitter that the Red Sox moved him to the outfield, and then sold him to the New York Yankees in 1920, a move that has haunted the Red Sox ever since. Ruth led the major leagues in home runs for ten seasons, and in 1927 established a home-run record of sixty for one season that would stand for more than three decades. It was finally broken by Roger Maris in 1961, who hit sixty-one homers in a 162-game season. Since Ruth had played a 154-game season, Maris's record was given an asterisk, but it was subsequently removed on the basis of the argument that the longer modern season was actually more difficult because of frequent air travel and the great shift from day to night games. In 1998, Maris's record was beaten by both Mark McGwire of the St. Louis Cardinals, who had seventy home runs, and by Sammy Sosa of the Chicago Cubs, who had sixty-six. In his entire career, Ruth hit 714 home runs, a record that was finally surpassed by Henry Aaron of the Atlanta Braves in 1974. While Ruth's records may have been topped, he remains the greatest legend in baseball.

142.

1927—THE FIRST ''DISC JOCKEY''

In 1927, Great Britain's radio broadcasting system, the BBC, which operated under a royal charter, began the first regular program of recorded music anywhere in the world. That means that the host of the show, one Christopher Stone, has the honor of being the world's first disc jockey, although the term would not come into use until the late 1930s in America. The initial BBC program played classical music, but the term "disc jockey" would eventually become largely associated with popular music. Nevertheless, Christopher Stone is regarded as the first of the breed.

143.

1928—HERBERT HOOVER ELECTED PRESIDENT

Herbert Hoover had been one of the few distinguished members of President Harding's Cabinet, and had continued as secretary of commerce through President Coolidge's full term as well. The economy was booming (although heading for the Great Crash), and Hoover's opponent was New York Governor Alfred E. Smith, the first Roman Catholic to be nominated for the presidency. Hoover beat Smith by 444 electoral votes to 87, and Smith even lost New York. But historians give him credit for starting the coalition that would back Franklin D. Roosevelt's New Deal four years later. Al Smith's appeal to labor and urban ethnic voters allowed him to carry the nation's twelve largest cities, all of which had gone for Coolidge four years earlier.

144.

1928—"STEAMBOAT WILLIE"

Steamboat Willie" was a cartoon short subject. It wasn't a work of great film art, but it did serve to introduce a character created by a young animator who had started out drawing cartoons for newspapers. The animator was Walt Disney, and the little black-and-white silent short introduced a character named Mickey Mouse. Few who saw that film in 1928 could have suspected that Disney would go on to produce the most famous entertainment company on the face of the planet, for which Mickey would become the chief symbol. Some people now complain about the "Disneyfication" of the world, but most families take endless delight in the full-length animated cartoons and the amusement parks that are Mickey's descendants. Seldom has so much come from such modest beginnings as "Steamboat Willie."

145.

1928—ANTIMATTER

Paul A. M. Dirac, the English physicist, worked out an equation to elucidate the relationship of Albert Einstein's theory of special relativity and quantum mechanics, the theory of subatomic particles based on the work of Max Planck in 1900, Einstein in 1905, Niels Bohr in 1913, and Werner Heisenberg in 1927 as well as that of numerous other top physicists. Dirac was horrified to discover, however, that his equation demanded the existence of a positively charged electron—in a word, antimatter. However, in 1932, using the cloud chamber at the California Institute of Technology, Carl D. Anderson isolated the positively charged electron. The recognition of the existence of antimatter has proved fundamental to modern physics and the bizarre world of quantum mechanics, which underlie the apparent "reality" of the Newtonian universe. What we apprehend with our senses, it has turned out, is only a small part of the story. Paul Dirac shared the 1933 Nobel Prize in Physics with Erwin Schrödinger, whose 1927 basic quantum equation was modified by Dirac's discovery.

146.

1928—ACADEMY AWARDS

On May 16, 1928, the elite of Hollywood, California, gathered at the Roosevelt Hotel for a dinner and self-congratulation. The newly formed Academy of Motion Picture Arts and Sciences was handing out its first awards, which immediately got the nickname "Oscars." There were only thirty-six tables and there was little tension, since the names of the winners had been announced in February. A flying movie, *Wings,* whose special effects can still impress, was Best Picture. Young Janet Gaynor was named Best Actress for her roles in three separate movies, the best remembered of which is *Seventh Heaven.* Emil Jannings won Best Actor for two films, but the German-born silent star was already on his way home to his native country, fleeing the sudden popularity of talking pictures. He did send a telegram, which was read by Douglas Fairbanks in his impeccable English accent: "I therefore ask you to kindly hand me now already the statuette award to me." This brought down the house, but also indicated why Fairbanks would have a career in sound movies and Jannings would not.

The general idea of the Academy Awards has been adopted by every entertainment medium in every major country since, but today's televised Oscars remain the most watched, seen around the world each year by more than two billion people.

147.

1929—THE ST. VALENTINE'S DAY MASSACRE

On Valentine's Day 1929, Al Capone dispatched a small group of his more than seven hundred goons to rub out a rival gang's leaders in a Chicago garage. This bloody massacre was only one of the hundreds of gang murders that took place every year in Chicago during Prohibition, when Capone controlled ten thousand speakeasies in that city alone. But the St. Valentine's Day Massacre became *the* shocking symbol of all that was wrong with Prohibition, and helped lead to its repeal in 1933. Capone was never convicted of murder, but he was finally imprisoned on tax-evasion charges in 1931. The federal government had seized much of his property, including his armored limousine. When the Japanese bombed Pearl Harbor on December 7, 1941, President Roosevelt scheduled a speech to Congress the next day to ask for a declaration of war. Fearful for Roosevelt's safety, the Treasury Department pulled out of mothballs the only armored car available for the president to ride in: Al Capone's limousine. Thus one of the most infamous gangsters of the century ended up providing the first armored vehicle ever used by a U.S. president.

148.

1929—''BLACK FRIDAY''

On October 29, 1929, the United States stock market crashed, ushering in the worldwide economic collapse known as the Great Depression. Twelve days earlier, America's foremost economist, Yale Professor Irving Fisher, had asserted: "Stocks have reached what looks like a permanently high plateau." There had been a scare on October 24, but the collapse on the twenty-ninth was catastrophic. What's more, the value of stocks kept going down until March 1933, when the new president, Franklin Delano Roosevelt, took the drastic step of closing all banks temporarily. Stocks had by then lost 80 percent of their value at the beginning of October 1929. Roosevelt got many new controls enacted by Congress, and more have followed since, especially those dealing with computerized trading. Supposedly, "Black Friday" can't happen again, but there are those who insist on recalling, from time to time, the optimistic words of Irving Fisher.

149.

1929—BYRD FLIES OVER SOUTH POLE

On November 29, 1929, Commander Richard E. Byrd of the United States Navy became the first man to fly successfully over both the North and South poles. Together with pilot Floyd Bennett, he had flown over the North Pole in May 1926, but the 1929 flight over the South Pole was regarded as more difficult. Byrd was promoted to admiral in 1930. That year, he set up a base, Little America, in Antarctica, from which he made five major explorations of that frozen continent, spending several months alone near the South Pole in 1933. His expeditions to Antarctica, the last of which took place in 1955–1956, are the primary basis for United States land claims on the continent.

150.

1929—THE MUSEUM OF MODERN ART

Privately endowed by such philanthropists as Mrs. John D. Rockefeller, and with a permanent collection based on the gift of her extraordinary collection by Lillie P. Bliss, the Museum of Modern Art opened its doors in New York City in 1929 with special exhibitions of works by Paul Cézanne, Paul Gauguin, Georges Seurat, and Vincent Van Gogh. Many other similar museums have been built around the world since, and traditional museums have in many cases supplemented their Old Masters with modern works, but the Museum of Modern Art remains the preeminent institution of its kind in the world. Its photography and film collections are also famous, and the museum led the way in collecting modern home furnishings that have acquired the status of art. MOMA, as it is often called, was also in the vanguard of the museum gift-shop concept, which plays an increasingly important role in augmenting income for museums around the world. While MOMA has serious rivals for the excellence of its collections, its development provided the template that other institutions have followed.

151.

1930—THE NINTH PLANET DISCOVERED

In 1915, the year before his death, Percival Lowell, the eminent American astronomer, had predicted the existence of a ninth planet, based on perturbations in the orbits of Neptune and Uranus that indicated the pull of another planet's gravity. Lowell had made one major mistake as an astronomer, claiming to see "canals" on Mars in 1894, but he was correct about the existence of Pluto. Working at the Lowell Observatory in Flagstaff, Arizona, which Lowell had helped to fund with his personal fortune and had headed in the last years of his life, Clyde W. Tombaugh finally managed to photograph Pluto on February 18, 1930, using a new wide-field camera he had developed. Although Pluto was found where Lowell said it would be, its mass does not fully explain the perturbations in the orbits of Neptune and Uranus, which has led many astronomers to believe that there must be a tenth planet, perhaps in an orbit that keeps it permanently hidden from us by the sun.

152.

1930—THE GRAND SLAM OF GOLF

The twentieth century has had many great golfers, from Ben Hogan to Arnold Palmer to Jack Nicklaus, but only one man was able to win the Grand Slam of Golf. In 1930, the Grand Slam consisted of the American and British Amateur Championships and the British and American Open Championships. All four were won by Bobby Jones, a lawyer from Atlanta. Jones was an amateur player who had already won each of the four Grand Slam events at least twice. After he captured them, he promptly retired at the age of twenty-eight from competitive golf. In those days the PGA Championship was played as a match tournament rather than a stroke tournament, and the Masters was not created until 1934. No single man has won all four contemporary Grand Slam events, the PGA, the Masters, and the British and American Opens in the same year, although Ben Hogan did capture three of them in 1953.

153.

1930—POPULATION EXPLOSION

When the population of the world passed two billion in 1930, the first warning cries about overpopulation were heard. By 1980, the world population had more than doubled and was expected to hit six billion by the turn of the century. Vast efforts, of varying kinds, have been made around the world to control the population explosion. In India and Africa, the rates are still climbing, but draconian measures in China, including mandatory abortion, have stemmed the tide there. In some areas of the world, particularly Western Europe, governments are actually beginning to worry aloud about population decline, on the grounds that not enough children are being born to support societies in which increasing longevity is creating an ever-greater number of elderly people.

154.

1930—THE WORLD CUP

The first World Cup in football (what Americans call soccer) was contested in 1930. Eleven nations competed in the matches held in Uruguay. Uruguay won the final against Argentina 4–2. The

World Cup competition has been held every four years since, except in 1942 and 1946, when interrupted by World War II. Today soccer is the most popular sport in the world, with more than twenty million participants, and the World Cup matches draw television audiences in excess of one billion viewers. Brazil is the only country to have played in all sixteen World Cup tournaments and has won four times, while Italy and West Germany each has had three victories. World Cup football, or soccer, was slow to catch on in the United States because of the popularity of its own kind of football, but the World Cup was held in the United States in 1994, and interest has been growing steadily.

155.

1931—A NATIONAL ANTHEM

The words to "The Star-Spangled Banner" were originally written by lawyer Francis Scott Key after watching the British bombard Fort McHenry in Baltimore Harbor in September 1814, during the War of 1812. The words were soon set to an old tune that was ironically of British origin, a popular pub song. President Woodrow Wilson made it the National Anthem by executive order in 1916, but the United States Congress did not confirm its status until it passed an act on March 3, 1931. The delay in congressional action was due to the fact that many people find "The Star-Spangled Banner" almost impossible to sing, and there have been efforts to replace it ever since, with "America the Beautiful" the most popular candidate. But because both that song and Irving Berlin's "God Bless America" have religious overtones, they raise constitutional issues. Even many people who can't sing "The Star-Spangled Banner" themselves do like to hear it sung by those who can negotiate its high notes.

156.

1931—NEVADA LEGALIZES GAMBLING

Taking a novel approach to a state fiscal crisis, Nevada legalized gambling in 1931, and encouraged the building of casinos. It also granted divorces following six weeks of residency. The two elements combined to make Nevada a mecca for pleasure-seekers and those in search of "quickie" divorces, or marriages, since no waiting period was required for a marriage license. Countless movies have been set in Las Vegas and Reno in the years since, ranging from silly comedies to 1996's grim, critically acclaimed *Leaving Las Vegas*, directed by Great Britain's Mike Figgis. Clare Booth Luce's play *The Women*, a huge Broadway hit in 1936 and later a movie, brought together a diverse set of women seeking quickie divorces in Reno, adding to the Nevada mystique. As divorce laws were made easier around the country in the second half of the century, Nevada lost out considerably on the divorce front, but its casinos still reign supreme, rivaled only by those of Atlantic City, New Jersey. In the 1990s, more and more states began legalizing gambling as a means of raising state income. Nevada was once known as the "sin state," but many would argue that it has turned out simply to be ahead of the times.

157.

1931—THE EMPIRE STATE BUILDING

The load-bearing iron-frame structure introduced in Chicago in 1885 by William LeBaron Jenney, together with the development of a safe passenger elevator by Elisha Otis, made possible the skyscraper, which would become the twentieth century's signature form of architecture. From New York's Flatiron Building of 1902, through the Empire State Building, completed in 1931 and for decades the tallest edifice in the world, to the World Trade Center and Chicago's Sears Tower, the byword in architecture has been "Can you top this?" But the Empire State Building has retained public affection as *the* emblematic skyscraper of the century. Its hold on the public has been much aided by Hollywood, which had King Kong knocking airplanes out of the air from its spire; Frank Sinatra, Gene Kelly, and Jules Munshin dancing on its observation deck in 1949's *On the Town*; and Tom Hanks and Meg Ryan finding

true love there in 1993's *Sleepless in Seattle*. The Empire State Building, in fact, seems destined to signify the American Century as the
Colosseum does imperial Rome.

158.

1931—THE BRITISH COMMONWEALTH OF NATIONS

Of all the great European imperial powers that ruled vast foreign domains down through the centuries, none could equal
the British Empire in the vastness of the colonial areas under its
control. The loss of the American colonies was only a small setback
to an empire that by the time of World War I, stretched from Canada to Africa to India and Australia. Great Britain also had the
strength and wisdom, in most cases, to loosen its grip and recon-
stitute the nature of its relationship with its colonial powers in
ways that preserved more influence than any other colonial power
was able to retain. The most important step in that regard was
taken in 1931, when the Statute of Westminster created the British
Commonwealth of Nations, in which countries around the world
were given independent and equal status under the Crown. There
are currently fifty-three members of the Commonwealth, of which
sixteen accept Queen Elizabeth II as head of state, including Canada
and Australia, the two largest member nations. South Africa, which
withdrew in 1961, rejoined the Commonwealth as apartheid came
to an end in 1994.

159.

1932 — FRANKLIN D. ROOSEVELT ELECTED
PRESIDENT

Roosevelt, a cousin of Theodore Roosevelt but a Democrat instead of a Republican, had run for vice president on the James Cox Democratic ticket in 1920. He had since contracted polio, fought his way back to health, and won two 2-year terms as governor of New York in 1928 and 1930. Roosevelt became the first presidential candidate to give an acceptance speech at his party's convention, and newsreel coverage, with the recent advent of sound, got his campaign off to a roaring start. He blamed the Republicans for the Great Depression that followed the crash of 1929 (which was in fact worldwide) and promised relief for the average person. Beating Hoover 472 electoral votes to 59, he used what was called the "Hundred Days" to push through the most astonishing array of new fiscal and social measures in American history, which came to be known as the New Deal.

160.

1932 — A DEPRESSION ANTHEM

Composer Jay Gouney and lyricist E. Y. Harburg wrote a song in 1932 that was to become emblematic of the Great Depression. "Brother, Can You Spare a Dime?," with its rhythmic lament for the loss of employment as a builder of the nation's greatness and its haunting title refrain, summed up the sense of despair that was felt by millions in those hard years. Properly sung, the song can still bring tears to the eyes of people who have never known hardship:

Once I built a railroad, made it run, made it race against
time . . .

Once I built a tower to the sun, brick and rivet and lime . . .

The expression of loss not only of work but of a sense of purpose is palpable. Along with Pete Seeger's 1960 elegy for the dream
of peace, "Where Have All the Flowers Gone?" and Bob Dylan's gen-
erational song of the 1960s, "Blowin' in the Wind," "Brother, Can
You Spare a Dime?" is one of the great social anthems of the century.

161.

1932 — MOBILES

The American artist Alexander Calder, born in Philadelphia in
1898, created a new art form in 1932 by constructing his first
mobiles, hanging sculptures with movable elements. Many other artists have since made use of the form, and even children learn to
construct them in art classes, but Calder's classic originals remain
among the important artworks of the century. Calder, who died in
1973, was honored in 1998 by the issuance of a set of U.S. first-class
postage stamps that showed a number of his mobiles. The extent of
his influence is demonstrated by the fact that the organizers of a
show of his mobiles, scheduled to travel to several American museums in 1998–1999, demanded that mobiles by other artists be removed from the gift shops of the participating museums.

162.

1932 — INTO THE STRATOSPHERE

In 1932, the French physicist Auguste Piccard became the first
person to ascend into the earth's stratosphere, 55,500 feet above
the surface, by balloon. Piccard (1884–1962), a Belgian who became

one of the century's most audacious explorers, also descended deep into the ocean in the late 1940s in a bathyscape (a submarine lowered by cable from a ship) of his own design. He lived to see his son Jacques who, together with U.S. Navy Lieutenant Don Walsh, in 1960 used another bathyscape to reach the deepest point of the world's oceans. This was the Marianas Trench, southwest of Guam in the Pacific, 38,000 feet below sea level. In one of its typical references to great scientific figures of the past, *Star Trek: The Next Generation* named the captain of the spaceship *Enterprise* Jean-Luc Picard in tribute to Auguste and Jacques Piccard.

To bring things full circle, on March 21, 1999, Dr. Bertrand Piccard, a Swiss psychiatrist and grandson of Auguste Piccard, completed the first successful flight around the globe by balloon. Bertrand Piccard and his British copilot, Brian Jones, had taken off from the Swiss Alps nineteen days earlier in their 180-foot-tall Breitling Orbiter 3 balloon. After circumnavigating the world, the two men landed three hundred miles southwest of Cairo, Egypt. As had been the case with his grandfather's ascent into the stratosphere, and his father's descent into the Marianas Trench, Bertrand Piccard would go into the record books for achieving something no human had done before.

163.

1933—THE CONCEPT OF THE CHAIN REACTION

Ernest Rutherford, who in 1901 had discovered the nature of radiation together with Frederick Soddy, unwisely stated in 1933 that atomic energy could not be utilized on the basis of present knowledge. This pronouncement by Lord Rutherford annoyed a young colleague named Leo Szilard, a Hungarian who had recently fled Hitler's Germany and was working in a laboratory at St. Bart's Hospital in London. Walking to work one morning, Szilard paused for a red light near St. Bart's. Before the light changed, his train of thought had brought him to one of the great "eureka" moments of twentieth-century science—the idea that if an atom was hit with sufficiently strong force by one neutron, the atom would break apart, releasing two neutrons. He immediately began calling this process a "chain reaction," and patented it in 1934. While waiting for a stoplight to change, Szilard had broken through to the secret of atomic energy. Working with Enrico Fermi and others on the Manhattan Project a decade later, he would see his idea made reality with the first controlled nuclear chain reaction, on December 2, 1942 (see Entry 210). The ability to create a controlled chain reaction made it possible for the new team headed by J. Robert Oppenheimer to build the first atomic bomb, which was exploded at White Sands, New Mexico, on July 16, 1945.

164.

1933—"FIRESIDE CHATS"

In 1933, President Roosevelt came up with a new way of communicating with the American people. He started regular "fireside chats" from the White House, broadcast nationwide on the radio. American presidents have been seeking new ways to cozy up to the American people ever since, as for example Jimmy Carter giving his famous speech from the White House on energy conservation while wearing a cardigan sweater, or Bill Clinton's mastery of the televised "town meeting" format. During much of the nineteenth century, presidential candidates didn't even go off on the hustings to make speeches; they would conduct "front porch campaigns" from their homes while surrogates made the speeches around the country. With the increasing domination of mass electronic media as the twentieth century has progressed, presidents have had to find new ways to connect with voters, and Roosevelt's "fireside chats" were the first step along the way.

165.

1933—*ULYSSES* ALLOWED INTO UNITED STATES

James Joyce's *Ulysses,* the huge experimental novel about a day in the life of the inhabitants of Dublin, Ireland, had originally been published in Paris in 1922. It had been banned immediately in the United States as obscene by the U.S. Post Office. A trial in New York in 1933 before federal Judge John M. Woolsey brought testimony from many eminent literary figures about the novel's importance as literature. Woolsey lifted the ban, calling the novel "a sincere and serious attempt to devise a new literary method for the observation and description of mankind." *Ulysses* was quickly published by Random House and arguably became the most influential novel of the century, despite its complex prose and symbolism. In 1988, the board of the Modern Library compiled a list of the century's hundred best novels, and *Ulysses* headed the list.

166.

1934—HITLER AS FÜHRER

At the end of January 1933, the president of Germany, aging World War I hero Field Marshal Paul von Hindenburg, found himself forced to appoint Adolf Hitler as chancellor of Germany. He loathed Hitler, whom he called "the Bavarian Corporal," but Hitler's Nazi party held the largest bloc of seats in the Reichstag (Parliament), 230 out of 608. In a politically divided and economically unstable country, Hindenburg had no choice. When Hindenburg died on August 2, 1934, Hitler proclaimed himself Führer, consolidating the posts of president and chancellor. He was backed by 88 percent of the voters. The Nazis were already in complete control, anyway, but now Hitler would be in a position to implement his plans for the ascendancy of the "master race" without hindrance.

167.

1934—THE LONG MARCH

Pressed on all sides by the forces of Nationalist Chinese leader General Chiang Kai-shek, the Red Army of China marched west and then north, led by Mao Tse-tung. There were ninety thousand men and women at the beginning of the Long March, but when it ended at Yenan in north-central China six thousand miles away and a year later, only half that number remained. After reestablishing themselves in Yenan, the Communists would join in fighting the Japanese during World War II, but civil war broke out again between the Nationalists and the Communists after 1945, and this time the Communists would win.

168.

1934—THE DUST BOWL

Prolonged drought in the south-central United States led to enormous dust storms that routed thousands of homesteaders from their small farms in 1934. Large numbers of them decided to migrate to the supposedly green paradise of California. Called "Okies" and "Arkies," after the states of Oklahoma and Arkansas that they were fleeing, these displaced persons traveled slowly across the country in old cars and wagons, stopping at makeshift camps along the way. Their plight became a symbol of the Great Depression, and their lives were indelibly captured by John Steinbeck in his novel *The Grapes of Wrath* and the great film that was made from it. Steinbeck won the Pulitzer Prize in 1940 for the novel, and John Ford won an Oscar for directing the movie, which was released in 1940. There had been other devastating droughts in American history, particularly in the nineteenth century, but the hardships that nature can inflict even in a country as rich as America were brought home in a new way during the Dust Bowl years of the 1930s.

169.

1935—NATIONAL LABOR RELATIONS ACT

New York Democratic Senator Robert Ferdinand Wagner, born in Germany, was the author of the National Labor Relations Act of 1935, which finally affirmed on the federal level the right of labor to organize and to engage in collective bargaining. The legislation is commonly referred to as the Wagner Act. Wagner, who was one of President Franklin D. Roosevelt's most trusted advisers in shaping the New Deal, also influenced the shape of the Social Security Act passed that same year (see next entry). The Wagner Act gave the American worker greater power to determine his or her economic standing as an employee, while the Social Security Act would provide a safety net during unemployment and in retirement. Many historians believe that Roosevelt might have chosen Wagner as his vice-presidential running mate in 1940 or 1944, but that was precluded by the Constitution on two counts: naturalized citizens are not eligible to become president, and the Constitution also specifies that the president and vice President must be from different states. Both Roosevelt and Wagner were New Yorkers.

170.

1935—SOCIAL SECURITY

One of the centerpieces of President Franklin D. Roosevelt's New Deal, the Social Security Act was passed by the United States Congress on August 14, 1935, creating a federal system of old age and survivor's insurance. Both employers and employees contributed to the fund, initially 1 percent of the worker's salary. The fund would pay out a monthly pension of up to $75 to those retiring at sixty-five. The original Act also provided grants to states to defray the costs of programs designed to help those who did not qualify under the federal plan. A joint federal and state system of unemployment compensation was also created, along with special provisions offering help to dependent mothers, the blind, the wheelchair-bound, and others. This was the beginning of the "entitlement programs" that were later expanded to include welfare, Medicare, Medicaid, and others. At the end of the century, many of these programs have become "hot button" political issues in a way that would no doubt astound Roosevelt and the Congress that passed the Social Security Act.

171.

1935—JOLIOT-CURIES WIN NOBEL PRIZE IN CHEMISTRY

Frederick Joliot and Irene Curie married in 1926. They took each other's names and became the Joliot-Curies. Irene was the daughter of the great pioneers of radioactive substances, Pierre and Marie Curie. They had jointly received the Nobel Prize in Physics in 1903, together with Antoine Becquerel, and Marie also was awarded the chemistry prize in 1911. A year after her mother's death, Irene Joliot-Curie would receive, along with her husband, the 1935 Nobel Prize in Chemistry for their work in the production of radioactive substances through bombardment by alpha particles. Irene Joliot-Curie was the first offspring of a Nobel Prizewinner to receive one herself.

172.

1935—ALCOHOLICS ANONYMOUS

Founded by two former alcoholics in 1935, AA became the prototype for many other recovery groups in succeeding decades. Although it has been criticized for its emphasis on religion, the organization has tens of thousands of functioning groups around the world, and has helped millions of people. The idea of group therapy has played a major role in twentieth-century societies, particularly in the United States. While earlier groups concentrated on helping people deal with problems like alcoholism and gambling, the AA concept has spread to include many kinds of groups, from cancer survivors to divorced people, and has been widely employed in criminal rehabilitation as well. The idea has also spawned many self-realization groups, usually led by "gurus," including such organizations as EST, which have often been controversial. Alcoholics Anonymous and similar recovery groups have for decades proved themselves a valuable resource for troubled people.

173.

1936—*LIFE* MAGAZINE

Picture magazines began to proliferate in the second half of the nineteenth century, but they were restricted to using drawings, often by important artists such as Frederic Remington. By the end of the 1800s, photographs were beginning to appear as well, but text continued to dominate illustrations until the launch of the publication *Life* by Henry Luce in 1936. The format was soon copied by magazines such as *Look* in the United States, and by many similar magazines in countries around the world. While *Life* sometimes published long prose pieces, including Ernest Hemingway's short novel *The Old Man and the Sea,* it was cherished for its pictures, taken by the world's greatest photographers. Picture magazines were eventually pushed aside by television, and *Life* itself continues in only a vestigial form, but for the forty midcentury years, *Life* conveyed the pulse of the times to more than five million readers a week.

174.

1936—SPANISH CIVIL WAR

The bloody three-year Spanish Civil War began in 1936 when General Francisco Franco led an army revolt in Morocco and then invaded his own Spanish homeland on the side of right-wing rebels. The Spanish Republic that had been formed in 1931 was overthrown in the process, and Franco would become the dictator of Spain from 1939 to his death in 1975. The war ostensibly pitted Nationalists against Loyalists, but there were strange bedfellows on both sides. Among the Nationalists were not only the Fascists, but also the landed aristocracy and the Roman Catholic Church. The Loyalists were made up not only of liberals and socialists, but also of Communists and anarchists, an even more unstable mixture. International brigades were formed by young volunteers from many countries to aid the Loyalists, an experience that would lead to such famous works of literature as George Orwell's *Homage to Catalonia* (1938) and Ernest Hemingway's *For Whom the Bell Tolls* (1940). Picasso's epic painting "Guernica" depicted the bombing of that Spanish town by the Fascists.

The Soviet Union aided the Loyalists militarily, but even greater resources were made available to the Nationalists by Hitler's Germany and Mussolini's Fascist Italy. The conflict thus became in many ways a rehearsal for World War II. With great cunning, Franco managed to maintain neutrality in World War II, and toward the end of his life made preparations for the restoration of a democratic monarchy. Franco remains a villain to many, but others claim that his long, repressive regime actually united Spain in a way that made democracy possible.

175.

1936—THE "NAZI OLYMPICS"

The Berlin Summer Olympics of 1936 provided Hitler a chance to show off the grandiose efficiency of his "new Germany" as well as to play genial host to the world's athletes, soft-pedaling his ambitions of conquest. Controversies from the Berlin Olympics still reverberate. Leni Riefenstahl's *Olympia*, which recorded the games in great detail, is widely regarded by critics as a great film, but her work has been forever tainted by the fact that she was Hitler's personal moviemaker and had earlier made an equally arresting movie about his Nuremberg rallies.

Another controversy centers on the great achievements of the American athlete Jesse Owens, who captured four gold medals at the Berlin Olympics. It is still often said that Owens's performance infuriated Hitler, since he was black and his victories gave the lie to Hitler's belief in German racial superiority. However, while this made excellent anti-Nazi propaganda, Jesse Owens himself said that Hitler shook his hand and congratulated him. Even so, the Berlin Olympics would be the last Games for ten years as Hitler's dreams of world domination plunged the globe into World War II.

176.

1936—ABDICATION OF EDWARD VIII OF GREAT BRITAIN

At the age of forty-one, Edward VIII became king of Great Britain in 1936. A man of great charm, he was popular with his subjects until he announced his intention of marrying an American woman named Wallis Warfield Simpson, who was in the process of divorcing for the second time. The British government, led by Prime Minister Stanley Baldwin, not only viewed marriage to a divorced woman as unacceptable, but saw Edward's insistence on doing so as a constitutional threat. In the background, there was concern about Edward's apparent sympathy for Hitler. While the successor next in line, Edward's younger brother, Albert George, was regarded as something of a lightweight and hampered by a stutter, he seemed a more fitting choice than a king married to a divorced American who was probably too old to have children. Edward VIII was forced to abdicate, and became the duke of Windsor;

he married Wallis Simpson two months after her divorce was finalized, in June 1937. George VI turned out to be just the right man for the hour, and helped lead his people through World War II with a calm fortitude that gained him their love and respect. His wife, Elizabeth, later the Queen Mother to Elizabeth II, became immensely popular as well.

177.

1936—ROOSEVELT REELECTED TO SECOND TERM

With New Deal legislation gradually improving the economy, and providing new hope for millions, President Roosevelt won a second term with the biggest landslide since James Monroe gained a second term in 1820. The Republican candidate was Kansas Governor Alfred Landon, who managed to keep his good humor even when he got only 8 electoral votes to Roosevelt's 523. Alf Landon's daughter would later reclaim some of her family's political honor; Nancy Landon Kassebaum would serve three terms as senator from Kansas. Roosevelt ran in 1936 for the second time with Texan John Nance Garner, who will always be remembered for his pithy assessment of his high office: the vice presidency, he said, "wasn't worth a pitcher of warm spit."

178.

1936—THE BROTHERHOOD OF
SLEEPING CAR PORTERS

In 1936, the American Federation of Labor granted a charter to the Brotherhood of Sleeping Car Porters, marking the first time that a union of African Americans was recognized. The Pullman

Company, which owned the sleeping cars, agreed to bargain with the new union the following year, in compliance with the Wagner Act of 1935. The recognition of this union helped to pave the way for the integration of the American union movement following World War II.

179.

1937—BURNING OF THE *HINDENBURG*

On May 6, 1937, the German passenger zeppelin *Hindenburg* arrived at its mooring tower in Lakehurst, New Jersey, after a transatlantic crossing. The 803-foot rigid airship, kept aloft by 7 million cubic feet of hydrogen gas in its cigar-shaped body, burst into flames, killing 15 passengers, 15 crew members, and 1 member of the ground crew; 62 people survived the tragedy.

The burning of the *Hindenburg* was the first transportation disaster caught on newsreel film, as well as by still photographers, as it took place. What's more, a radio reporter named Herbert Morrison was recording a story about the airship's arrival for later broadcast. His famous cry, "Oh, the humanity!" as bodies tumbled from the burning craft was the precursor of many an eyewitness disaster report. The sensation caused by the burning of the *Hindenburg* is the root of today's on-the-scene disaster reporting on the evening television news. From that moment on, it seemed that the public could never get enough of this kind of report.

180.

1937—AMELIA EARHART DISAPPEARS IN PACIFIC

In 1928, at the age of thirty, Amelia Earhart had become the first woman to fly the Atlantic, together with copilot Wilbur Stultz and mechanic Louis "Slim" Gordon. Earhart immediately became one of the most famous women on Earth. She made a solo transatlantic flight in 1932, and in 1935 became the first person of either sex to make a solo flight from Hawaii to California. In the summer of 1937, she and copilot Frederick J. Noonan set off on a round-the-world flight, but their plane disappeared on July 2 between New Guinea and Howland Island. Since there was no radio dispatch indicating any trouble, and because the wreckage of the plane was never found, Earhart's disappearance took its place as one of the great mysteries of the century. There was speculation that she might have been shot down by the Japanese, and the relationship between herself and Noonan even gave rise to the notion that they had deliberately vanished. As famous in her time as any woman of the century has been, Amelia Earhart remains a legend and her disappearance an enigma.

181.

1938 — XEROXING

Physicist Chester Carlson invented the prototype of the photo-copy machine in 1938. Unlike the mimeograph machine, it used no ink, but instead made use of static electricity. A charged plate was suffused with light, which removed the electric charge from the white areas, while a plastic powder called toner was applied to the remaining areas, with the resulting printout reproducing the original.

Carlson called his new process "xerography," from a combi-nation of Greek words that literally meant "dry writing." It took another nine years to refine the process and bring down its cost to the point that it was commercially viable. But it was not until 1959, with the founding of the Xerox Corporation, that photocopying be-came the true wave of the future.

182.

1938 — THE HOUSE UN-AMERICAN ACTIVITIES COMMITTEE

Organized by Congressman Martin Dies of Texas, the HUAC would have a disproportionate effect on the politics of the nation over the next two decades. Plenty of politicians and com-mentators had been frothing at the mouth about the dangers of communism since the early 1920s (although even the conservative press lord William Randolph Hearst had initially applauded the Russian Revolution and the ideas of Lenin). The rise of fascism and nazism in Europe in the 1930s gave new cause for alarm, and HUAC became the first formal government entity to focus on the threat of communism and fascism, using its subpoena power to investigate Americans suspected of being "foreign dupes." HUAC would give rise to the full-fledged "red scare" of the 1950s and the excesses of McCarthyism.

It was HUAC that conducted the hearings on communism in the entertainment industry during the 1950s, while the McCarthy hearings focused on the infiltration of the government by Communists. The entertainment-industry hearings led to the blacklisting of dozens of Hollywood, television, and stage performers, writers, and directors, in some cases because they had refused to name friends and acquaintances as Communists, in others simply because the fact that they had been called to testify made them "too controversial" to employ. Among the famous people blacklisted in the 1950s were actress Anne Revere, who had won the Supporting Actress Oscar for *National Velvet* in 1945; director Joseph Losey, who moved to England and made such famous films as 1963's *The Servant;* and writer Dalton Trumbo, who in 1956 would win a Best Motion Picture Story Oscar for *The Brave One,* under the pseudonym Robert Rich.

183.

1938—"PEACE IN OUR TIME"

On September 30, 1938, the British prime minister, Neville Chamberlain, stood in front of 10 Downing Street and waved a piece of paper. The paper was the agreement he had just signed with Adolf Hitler in Munich, which was intended to solve the problem of Germany's insistent claims on Czechoslovakia. The solution, which had been suggested by Chamberlain himself, called for the annexation by Germany of those areas where more than 50 percent of the population approved of it. This meant that Germany gained control of the industrial heart of Czechoslovakia, the Sudetenland, with a population of nearly 3 million Sudeten Germans as well as 800,000 Czechs. The French had also been party to the agreement in Munich, which was meant to avert war but simply gave Hitler the security to become more aggressive. Winston Churchill, who had been shut out of Chamberlain's government, immediately issued a statement saying, "Britain and France had to choose between war and dishonor. They chose dishonor. They will have war." He was, of course, exactly right.

184.

1938—POLYTETRAFLUORETHYLENE

This is one of those unpronounceable chemical substances that was given a name by clever marketing people under which it became a household word. The word became so commonly used, in fact, that it was applied to Ronald Reagan to describe how charges against him never seemed to stick. Yes, the word is Teflon.

Discovered almost accidentally by DuPont chemist Dr. Roy Plunkett, Teflon was put to use in a wide variety of industrial processes in which its nonstick properties were extremely useful. It took a Frenchman named Mark Gregoire, however, to conceive of using it on cookware, which was first marketed in Europe under the name T-Fal. DuPont quickly entered the same market in the United States, and by the late 1960s, Teflon-coated pans were on their way to becoming a necessity in the American kitchen.

185.

1939—NEW YORK WORLD'S FAIR

As war clouds gathered over Europe, President Roosevelt presided at the opening of the New York World's Fair on April 30, 1939. Built in Flushing Meadows in Queens, the vast fair was anchored by a Court of Peace, a hopeful but futile tribute to the possibility of brotherhood among nations. The fair was famous for its towering Trylon and the huge crystal ball called the Perisphere. The exhibits at the fair prefigured many of the developments that would take place in technology and city planning in the second half of the century, from television to suburban sprawl.

186.

1939—HITLER INVADES POLAND

On August 31, 1939, Adolf Hitler broadcast peace proposals supposedly aimed at Poland, but they had not in fact been presented to Polish diplomats. That night German troops faked attacks on their own outposts on the Polish border, and in "retaliation" fifty-three German divisions smashed into Poland on September 1. The British and the French, which had signed a guarantee to protect Poland the previous year, took twenty-four hours to send Germany ultimatums to withdraw. With no answer forthcoming, Great Britain, Australia, and New Zealand declared war on Germany on September 3, and the French quickly followed suit. World War II had begun.

187.

1939 — BLACK HOLES

Before he became head of the Manhattan Project team of scientists that developed the atomic bomb, J. Robert Oppenheimer had written a 1939 paper positing the existence of a star of great size that could eventually collapse so completely, with its mass condensed to such small size, that its enormous gravity would not even allow light to escape from it. This paper met with a great deal of scorn. One of the debunkers of the idea was the American physicist John Archibald Wheeler. But Wheeler was eventually won over to the degree that he gave the name we know these stars by: black holes. Wheeler coined the term in 1969, and in the thirty years since, the study of black holes has been central to the extraordinary theoretical developments in the field of astrophysics, providing insight into how very peculiar the universe really is. Recently, several black holes have been physically confirmed to exist by advanced computer analysis, even though the objects cannot be seen.

188.

1939 — NYLON STOCKINGS

Nylon stockings were first demonstrated to the public at the 1939 New York World's Fair, and they were put on the market May 15, 1940. Nylon itself had been invented by an organic chemist named Wallace Carothers who was under contract to E. I. DuPont de Nemours and Company. He produced the synthetic fabric in 1935, after seven years' work. By the time nylons went on sale, advertised as "strong as steel and delicate as a spider's web," DuPont had invested $27 million in the new product. In the beginning, nylons were expensive and, because of World War II, hard to get hold of, so women treated them as though they were silk. But as the price went down in the postwar years, they became so ubiquitous as to be almost disposable items. It is doubtful that most women fully recognize that they are wearing a miracle: each stocking is manufactured from a single filament that is four miles in length and woven into three million loops.

189.

1939—FIRST COMMERCIAL
TRANSATLANTIC FLIGHT

Although transatlantic military flights had become increasingly common in the late 1930s, the first commercial flight from New York to London took place in June 1939. The Pan American flight cost about what a steamship crossing did at the time, $375 for a one-way ticket, and $675 round trip. With Germany's invasion of Poland in September 1939, commercial flights to Europe were suspended until after the war, when they would become so common as to all but eliminate luxury-liner transatlantic crossings by the mid-1970s. Eventually oceangoing vessels of somewhat smaller size offered vacation cruises in the Caribbean, the Mediterranean, and other areas around the world, but in the second half of the century, planes became the primary mode of long-distance passenger transportation.

190.

1939—HOLLYWOOD'S GREATEST YEAR

Among the classic movies that were *not* nominated for Best Picture in Hollywood's greatest year were *Beau Geste, Drums Along the Mohawk, Gunga Din, Juarez, Intermezzo,* and *The Private Lives of Elizabeth and Essex.* In that era, ten films were nominated for Best Picture rather than the five selected now, a tradition that began in 1944. The ten nominees in 1939 were: *Dark Victory, Gone With the Wind* (which won), *Goodbye, Mr. Chips, Love Affair, Mr. Smith Goes to Washington, Ninotchka, Of Mice and Men, Stagecoach, The Wizard of Oz,* and *Wuthering Heights.* This was Hollywood at its absolute peak.

191.

1939—THE HELICOPTER

Sometimes a concept takes an exceptionally long time to be turned into reality. In 1483, Leonardo da Vinci drew a sketch of a flying machine that is clearly a helicopter. Over the centuries, many inventors tried to make such a machine, and the efforts intensified after the first airplane flights of the Wright brothers. Success, however, eluded well-known English, French, Spanish, and German inventors. The problem was finally solved in 1939 by the Russian-American engineer Igor Sikorsky, who had designed and flown the first multiengined plane in 1913. Helicopters saw some use in World War II, but really came into play in the Korean War. In Vietnam, they were essential to American efforts in dealing with an essentially guerrilla enemy. In civilian life, helicopters have become an integral part of modern commerce and governmental activities, allowing rapid transport into and out of congested or dangerous areas.

192.

1940—THE RETREAT FROM DUNKIRK

In April 1940, Denmark, which had declared neutrality, surrendered to German troops; only a few Allied fighters were holding out in the mountains of Norway; and France was almost entirely in German hands. Several hundred thousand Allied troops—British, French, Belgians, and Poles—were trapped at Dunkirk, the French port on the North Sea. From May 26 to June 4, 1940, a flotilla of ships ranging from destroyers to fishing boats ferried 340,000 soldiers to safety in Great Britain, 200,000 of them British and 110,000 French. Winston Churchill called it a "miracle of deliverance," and British Poet Laureate John Masefield added a phrase to the English language when he termed the rescue a "nine days' wonder."

193.

1940—THE BATTLE OF BRITAIN

On July 10, 1940, the German Luftwaffe began bombing British coastal towns from the air. At this point, the British had only 1,450 pilots to the Germans' 10,000, but they were turning out new planes at the rate of 500 a month, twice the number the Germans were able to manufacture. The British, operating from a home base, and an island one at that, were in a better strategic position and also were able to make use of a new invention, radar.

London was first subjected to air attacks on September 7, and a bomb hit Buckingham Palace, which the royal family had refused to leave, on September 10. They were safe and their courage gave renewed spirit to the British resistance. The Battle of Britain came to an end on October 31, when Hitler decided that he was losing too many planes to British flyers. To this day, the Royal Air Force pilots, supplemented by Canadian and American volunteers, who fought the Battle of Britain in the skies over the English Channel and the North Sea are known as "the Few." This name stems from Winston Churchill's statement "Never in the field of human conflict was so much owed by so many to so few."

194.

1940—ROOSEVELT ELECTED TO UNPRECEDENTED THIRD TERM

George Washington had declined a third term as president, and no president had sought one since. In 1940, Roosevelt never announced he was running, but allowed the Democrats to nominate him anyway—just as he had planned. With Hitler rampaging across Europe, the public was in no mood for unknown quantities in the White House, even though the Republicans offered a very appealing candidate in businessman and political neophyte Wendell L. Willkie. John Nance Garner did not want another term as vice president, so for that post Roosevelt selected his secretary of agriculture, Henry A. Wallace, who was liked by farmers. This election wasn't quite the walkover the first two had been, but Roosevelt still won by a landslide, 449 electoral votes to Willkie's 82.

195.

1940—THE MAGNETRON

While the name "magnetron" sounds like something out of a 1930s pulp science-fiction story, this electronic tube was invented by a team of British researchers in 1940 at the University of Birmingham. Initially used in radar, the tube generated microwaves. In the early 1950s, it was discovered at the Raytheon Company that the magnetron was capable of melting chocolate that just happened to be in the pocket of a company researcher. This accidental discovery led to the development of microwave ovens, commercially introduced in 1955, which are now an integral part of food preparation in homes and restaurants around the world.

196.

1940—LEND-LEASE

On December 17, 1940, as war raged in Europe, President Roosevelt announced a new program to help the British while staying out of the actual war. He called the program Lend-Lease, and compared it to lending a neighbor a hose to put out a fire at his home, which would also help to ensure that the blaze wouldn't spread to his own property. The program would make it possible for Great Britain to buy food and raw materials from the United States without paying for them until the war was over. Fiercely opposed by Republican isolationists, it was guided through Congress by the new secretary of war, Henry L. Stimson, a Republican himself, whom Roosevelt had appointed in June 1940. The bill finally passed on March 11, 1941, and has often been called one of the greatest acts of generosity ever made by one nation to another.

197.

1940—THE BLOOD BANK

A medical institution that has saved millions of lives, the blood bank was originated in New York City in 1940 by Dr. Richard Charles Drew. But Dr. Drew was forbidden to donate his own blood to the institution he founded. Why? He was black.

198.

1941—THE SIEGE OF LENINGRAD

Although Hitler and Stalin had signed a nonaggression pact in 1939, and agreed to divide up several European countries, including Poland, Finland, and the smaller Lithuania, Latvia, and Estonia, Stalin was rightly suspicious of Hitler's long-term plans. Germany did indeed invade Russia along a thousand-mile front on June 22, 1941. By September 8, the German Army had completely surrounded Leningrad (formerly St. Petersburg), and the siege of that city would last nine hundred days in one of the most extraordinary standoffs in world history. More than one million citizens of Leningrad would eventually die from malnutrition or outright starvation, but some supplies reached the city across Lake Lagoda, on the shores of which Leningrad was built. Even in winter, once the ice on the lake had frozen to a depth of six feet, trucks could make their way across the surface. The heroism of the people of Leningrad is one of the great stories of the century, and the city was never captured by the Germans.

199.

1941—MARIAN ANDERSON SINGS AT THE LINCOLN MEMORIAL

The American contralto Marian Anderson had been told by the legendary conductor Arturo Toscanini in the 1930s, "A voice like yours comes but once in a century." But Marian Anderson was a black woman, and the United States was not yet ready for black opera singers. In 1941, however, she booked Constitution Hall in Washington, D.C., to give a concert. The hall was owned by the

DAR (the Daughters of the American Revolution), a patriotic society founded in 1890, and the organization canceled the concert as soon as it was informed about it. At this point, Walter White of the NAACP informed First Lady Eleanor Roosevelt about what was going on, and she called up the secretary of the interior (and her husband's most trusted adviser), Harold Ickes, to relay White's suggestion that an outdoor concert be held on government property, with the Lincoln Memorial as the obvious site. With President Roosevelt's approval, Ickes, whose Cabinet department was in charge of the Lincoln Memorial, made the arrangements. An audience of 75,000 gathered, including most of the foreign diplomatic corps. Miss Anderson opened with "America," and closed with "Nobody Knows the Trouble I've Seen," with opera arias in between. It has been described by people who were there as the most moving outdoor event ever held in Washington until the day in 1963 when Martin Luther King, Jr., gave his "I have a dream . . ." speech. Even so, it would not be until 1955, when she was fifty-three, that Marian Anderson became the first African American to sing at the Metropolitan Opera in New York.

200.

1941—MOUNT RUSHMORE MEMORIAL COMPLETED

Presidents Washington, Jefferson, Lincoln, and Theodore Roosevelt gaze out across South Dakota from Mount Rushmore, their gigantic visages a wonder of the modern world as the Colossus of Rhodes was of the ancient. The American sculptor John Gutzon Borglum, of Danish descent, designed and directed the vast project, employing 350 mostly local miners and quarrymen. Begun in 1927, the monument took fourteen years to complete and was dedicated in 1941, soon after Borglum's death. The final touches were supervised by his son Lincoln, who had worked on the project as a boy of fifteen.

201.

1941—MASS PRODUCTION OF PENICILLIN

Alexander Fleming had discovered penicillin in 1928, and in 1929 he wrote an article that stated, "It is suggested that it may be an efficient antiseptic for application to, or injection into, areas infected with penicillin-sensitive microbes." That single sentence would assure him an eventual share of a Nobel Prize. At the time, however, Fleming was unable to produce penicillin in doses concentrated enough to test its efficacy as an antibiotic. In the late 1930s, at Oxford University, the Australian-born bacteriologist Howard Florey, working with a young German refugee, Ernst Chain, were able to use new techniques, including freeze-drying, to produce penicillin in large enough quantities to reveal its astonishing ability to kill staphylococcal bacilli. In 1941, a crash program began to produce large amounts of penicillin for use on the battlefields of World War II. Much of this work was done at the U.S. Department of Agriculture laboratory in Peoria, Illinois. During World War I, enormous numbers of soldiers had died from staph infections that attacked even relatively minor wounds, but the advent of penicillin prevented the repeat of such tragic losses. Countless civilian lives would later be saved because of this "miracle drug." Fleming, Florey, and Chain shared the 1945 Nobel Prize for Physiology or Medicine for their work in the discovery and development of penicillin.

202.

1941—THE ATTACK ON PEARL HARBOR

Entire books have been written about the complex events that unfolded in the days preceding the Japanese bombing of the huge U.S. naval base at Hawaii's Pearl Harbor on December 7, 1941. The United States knew that as negotiations in Washington with Japanese diplomats foundered, an attack in the Pacific was likely, but it was thought probable that the Philippines would be the target. The United States had cracked the Japanese code, but the decoding of a crucial message was delayed. Army Chief of Staff George Marshall was one of the few who suspected that Pearl Harbor might be the target, but a warning he dispatched ended up being sent by Western Union because of static on military lines, and it arrived, by bicycle messenger, after the attack was over. The commanders at Pearl Harbor had misunderstood the import of other messages, and had U.S. planes lined up on the ground like ducks in a shooting gallery. In fact, so many small things went wrong, the situation resembled the classic rhyme about "for want of a shoe, a horse was lost," leading to the loss of an army and a kingdom. The devastation of Pearl Harbor, which included the loss of 5 battleships and 10 other smaller ships, as well as 188 planes and 2,400 men, half of them from the battleship *Arizona*, could have been even worse if a third strike by the Japanese had not been called off.

The following day, President Roosevelt spoke before Congress, describing the Pearl Harbor attack as "a day that will live in infamy," and asked for a declaration of war against Japan. The United States was now in World War II, and on the other side of the Atlantic Winston Churchill slept what he would later call "the sleep of the saved."

203.

1941—THE UNITED NATIONS

Woodrow Wilson had won the Nobel Peace Prize in 1919 for his work in establishing the League of Nations, but the organization had never been joined by the United States because of the opposition of isolationist senators. Without American participation, the League failed to deal with the rise of fascism in Europe and the expansionism of Japan in the Far East. It collapsed with the outbreak of World War II. President Franklin Delano Roosevelt and Prime Minister Winston Churchill revived the idea of an international body to settle disputes, discussing it at length during Churchill's Christmas stay at the White House in 1941. It was Roosevelt who came up with the name United Nations. Eager to suggest it to Churchill, Roosevelt arrived in his wheelchair at the door of his guest early on the morning of January 1, 1942, knocked, and was told to come in. A stark-naked Churchill, fresh from a bath, enthusiastically accepted the name, noting that the phrase was used in a poem by Lord Byron. A meeting of foreign ministers from twenty-six countries embraced the idea, as well as the name, that very day. The complete charter was drawn up in San Francisco in September 1945, and its headquarters were subsequently established in New York City.

204.

1942—THE "FINAL SOLUTION"

Persecution of German Jews had begun as soon as Hitler became chancellor of Germany. After he proclaimed himself Führer, the "Nuremberg Laws" were announced in September 1935, which stripped Jews of their few remaining civil rights—they had already been removed from public employment and driven out of the medical and legal professions. Much worse was to come. At a meeting on January 20, 1942, in Berlin, Hitler launched a new program called the "Final Solution," calling for the extermination of the Jews. Adolf Eichmann was put in charge. That spring, five camps devoted to the extermination of Jews became operational: Auschwitz, Chelmno, Treblinka, Sobibor, and Bergen-Belsen. A site at Dachau had been used as a prison for Hitler's political enemies when he was still only chancellor in 1933. It, too, was converted for use as a death camp. Auschwitz, the most infamous of all the camps, was alone capable of killing twelve thousand human beings a day.

205.

1942—JAPANESE INTERNMENT CAMPS IN THE UNITED STATES

On February 19, 1942, President Roosevelt signed an executive order that ended with 112,000 Japanese Americans, two thirds of them naturalized or native-born Americans, being rounded up and placed in internment camps for the remainder of the war. This move was supported by a broad array of distinguished Americans, including the newspaper columnist Walter Lippmann, California

Governor Earl Warren, and Supreme Court Justice Hugo Black. Astonishingly, one of the few important figures to tell Roosevelt it was wrong was FBI Director J. Edgar Hoover. Earl Warren would later say that it was the one thing in his career he was ashamed of.

In contradiction to the internment policy, eight thousand Japanese Americans, many drafted and some volunteers, served in the U.S. armed forces during World War II, many with great distinction.

206.

1942 — ''I SHALL RETURN''

In March of 1942, the Philippine Islands were on the verge of falling to the Japanese. When General Douglas MacArthur, the commander in the Philippines, was ordered to leave for Australia on March 12, 1942, to take command of all Allied forces in Southeast Asia, he uttered one of the most famous remarks of the war: "I shall return." And indeed he did, but it would be almost three years later.

207.

1942 — THE BATTLE OF MIDWAY

Admiral Isoroku Yamamoto, who had planned the attack on Pearl Harbor, devised a new plan in June 1942 to completely cripple American naval forces in the Pacific. Half his fleet was ordered to attack American-held Midway Island, with the other half held in reserve to attack whatever force was then dispatched from Pearl Harbor to assist. Having cracked the Japanese code, the U.S. forces were able to develop a hurried counterattack. Although the

United States lost twice as many planes (307 to 150 for the Japanese), Japan sacrificed 3,500 men to only 5 for the U.S., and 322 ships to only 2 American vessels. Although the war in the Pacific would last another three years, the Japanese never fully recovered from the terrible losses at Midway. It would be one of the most crucial engagements in the entire Pacific war.

208.

1942—THE BATTLE OF ALAMEIN

From October 23 to November 3, 1942, Britain's General Bernard Montgomery attacked El Alamein in North Africa, where the troops of "the Desert Fox," Germany's Field Marshal Erwin Rommel, were positioned. Rommel had been defeating British and Allied forces in North Africa for a year and a half with his brilliant improvisational moves, but the methodical Montgomery finally got the better of him at Alamein, and Rommel returned to Germany shortly afterward to try to persuade Hitler to give up on North Africa altogether. Hitler refused, to his cost, since he would be sacrificing troops in a losing cause in North Africa that he could have used elsewhere. The Allied victory in North Africa was crucial to plans for the invasion of Italy, which could not have been carried out while the Germans controlled the Mediterranean between Italy and North Africa.

Rommel would later be part of a plot formed by German officers to kill Hitler. As the greatest and most popular German general of the century, Rommel was not arrested, but he was informed by the S.S. that he would be tried unless he killed himself, which he did on October 14, 1944.

209.

1942—THE JEEP

Introduced in 1942, the jeep was given many nicknames by the Allied forces, including "The Iron Pony," "Leaping Lena," and "Panzer Killer." Its speed, and its maneuverability over almost any kind of terrain, made it the kind of secondary military tool that ultimately wins wars. It was a crucial "nail" in the Allied military machine, and a triumph of American car know-how. After the war, jeeps would be put to numerous peacetime uses, employed by ranchers, beach-safety patrols, park rangers, and many others who needed a vehicle that was reliable in rough terrain. In the 1990s, the financial resurgence of the Chrysler Corporation was greatly aided by the popularity of the suburban passenger vehicles produced by its Jeep division.

210.

1942—CONTROLLED CHAIN REACTION

On December 2, 1942, in a squash court under the football stadium at the University of Chicago, a team of scientists set in motion the first controlled chain reaction of atomic materials. The three most important of these Manhattan Project physicists were Enrico Fermi, Leo Szilard, and Arthur H. Compton. Italian-born Fermi had fled Europe with his Jewish wife, Laura, directly after receiving the Nobel Prize in Physics in Stockholm in 1938. Szilard, a Hungarian, had fled Hitler's Germany in 1933 for London and then emigrated to the United States in the same year that Fermi arrived in America. Compton, an American who won the physics Nobel in 1923, was the head of this first stage of the Manhattan

Project. When they knew they had succeeded, Compton called President Roosevelt's science adviser, James B. Conant, who would later become president of Harvard University, and told him, in prearranged code, that "Columbus has arrived in the New World." Conant asked how the natives were behaving, and Compton replied that they were calm, indicating that the chain reaction was entirely under control.

A new world had indeed been reached, but never again would it be possible to say that the consequences of atomic energy were entirely under control.

211.

1942—"ROSIE THE RIVETER"

As the United States drastically increased the drafting of young men to serve in the armed forces, their places were taken on assembly lines by American women. The number of women in the U.S. workforce would increase by 50 percent in the course of the war. Given the popular name "Rosie the Riveter," the female factory worker became commonplace, and contributed enormously to the U.S. war effort. Among these young women was a certain Norma Jean Baker, who got a job as a paint sprayer at a California defense plant. A photographer from the GI newspaper *Stars and Stripes* showed up at the plant to do a story on its women workers. The photograph of Norma Jean Baker that accompanied the story led to modeling jobs for her and started the career of the woman who would later become Marilyn Monroe. Although Marilyn's career was launched in a defense plant, most women would return to being homemakers once the war was over and the GIs came home to take up their factory jobs again. Even so, historians of the women's rights movement view the wartime experience of all those "Rosie the Riveters" as a crucial element in the development of the feminist movement in subsequent decades. Millions of young women had been given a taste of independence during the war that would change the way they looked at the world.

212.

1943—THE LOSS OF A STAR

On January 24, 1943, Nazi fighter planes shot down a British plane that they believed was carrying Winston Churchill back from his twelve days of meetings with President Roosevelt in the fabled and recently recaptured North African city of Casablanca. But the plane was carrying the actor Leslie Howard, who was returning from a secret mission to the governments of Spain and Portugal, during which he tried to persuade them to enter the war on the side of the Allies. The star of *The Scarlet Pimpernel* (1935), *Pygmalion* (1938), and *Gone With the Wind* (1939) was one of the most beloved actors in the world, and his death brought a wider and more deeply felt outpouring of grief than that of any nonmilitary person in the course of the war. To millions, Howard was a symbol of gallantry, and his loss hit extremely hard. The death of band leader Glenn Miller at the end of 1944, in an air crash while on his way to entertain troops, would have a special impact on Americans, but Howard had been loved not just in the United States and Great Britain but across Europe, in Australia, and in the British colonies around the world. Many newspaper headlines were variations on SCARLET PIMPERNEL KILLED.

213.

1943—THE PENTAGON

The Pentagon, headquarters of the United States Department of Defense in Arlington, Virginia, was the largest office building in the world when it was completed in 1943, and it remains so. The complex is actually five concentric buildings occupying a total of 4 acres, with 6,500,000 square feet of enclosed floor space for 23,000 workers. Because of both its size and security restrictions, there are believed to be only a handful of people who have ever seen all of it. Its very name is an instant reminder around the world of the military might of the United States.

214.

1943—THE BATTLE OF KURSK

The confrontation between the German and Russian armies around the small city of Kursk in Ukraine, which lasted from July 5 to July 12, 1943, was the greatest tank battle in the history of the world. Germany, which had lost the Battle of Stalingrad to the Russians at the end of January, had a force of nearly two million men at Kursk, opposed by a slightly larger Russian army. The battle was fought at such close quarters that the air forces on both sides became irrelevant; they could not bomb the enemy without killing their own men as well. In addition, it was almost impossible to see the battlefield from the air, so dense was the smoke from burning tanks. When it was over, the defeated Germans had lost so many men and armaments that they would be unable to mount a major offensive again. Like Napoleon before him, Hitler met with nothing but grief in the vastness that was Russia.

215.

1943—SUPERFORTRESS B-29S

The development of military aircraft took a great leap forward during World War II, with both the Allies and the Axis powers creating superb planes. But the one that is credited with winning the war for the Allies is the American B-29, introduced in 1943. With great range and large bomb capacity, these planes were crucial to the effort to retake the widely scattered Pacific islands occupied by the Japanese. And it was a stripped down B-29, named the *Enola Gay* after the pilot's mother, that dropped the first atomic bomb on Hiroshima on August 6, 1945.

More than sixteen million Americans were involved in some aspect of the production of B-29s from 1942 until the end of the war—the most colossal manufacturing effort ever undertaken in the history of humankind.

216.

1943—ITALY SWITCHES SIDES

On October 13, 1943, Italy declared war on its original ally, Germany. In July, Mussolini had been arrested by his own Fascist party and replaced with Marshal Pietro Badoglio. The Germans rescued Mussolini, who was then personally instructed by Hitler to set up a new regime in northern Italy. Mussolini was in fact going mad, and quite incapable of organizing anything. The Italian government had surrendered to Allied forces after the successful invasion of Sicily in early September, but Germany was determined to hold on to what Churchill had called "the soft underbelly of Europe," and fought the Allied forces (American, British, Australian, and Polish) mile by mile up the boot of Italy. War-weary Italians welcomed the Allies and the government switched sides, but it would take another ten months for the Allies to move as far north as Florence.

217.

1 9 4 4 — D - D A Y

The D-day invasion of Europe, on the sixth of June 1944, by the Allied forces massed on the coast of England, had been in preparation for over a year. Elaborate efforts were undertaken to throw the Nazis off the track, with references to an Operation Fortitude, to be headed by General George S. Patton, inserted into real dispatches and made the subject of false ones. This invasion was supposedly going to be launched across the English Channel to the sandy beaches of the Pas de Calais area. But the real invasion area was the beaches of Normandy, more difficult to land on but also more difficult to defend.

There were 6,483 ships and landing craft assembled on the British coast in the weeks before D-day, more than 4,000 of them landing craft, and there were 12,000 planes, of which 5,000 were fighters, amassed for air support. The invasion was supposed to take place on June 4, but was delayed for two days because of bad weather. A total of 23,000 men stormed the beaches of Normandy. American casualties on the first day were more than 4,600, with the largest number wounded or killed at Omaha Beach, which had the most difficult terrain and the best German divisions in place. Once the landing had been made, command of the ground forces was turned over to General Bernard Montgomery, even though there were considerably more American than British troops under his command. This was part of the agreement with the British that had made General Dwight D. Eisenhower Supreme Commander, but also sensibly reflected Montgomery's success against the armored divisions of Erwin Rommel in North Africa.

218.

1 9 4 4 — T H E   V - 1   R O C K E T

Hitler immediately retaliated for the Normandy invasion by un-
leashing a rain of terror on England in the form of bomb-laden
V-1 rockets. More than eighteen thousand were launched against
England between June 13 and September 8, only about half of
which the British were able to shoot down or explode before they
hit. The V-1s, and the V-2s used at the end of the war, were far
ahead of anything the Allies had developed in the way of rockets,
which was why German rocket scientists like Wernher von Braun
were brought to America after the war. Ironically, the United States
had one of the foremost rocket experimenters right at home in the
person of Robert H. Goddard. But although a German spy had reported his work back to Hitler, Goddard had been largely derided
in the United States, and would die at the age of sixty-three in
1945. Two decades later, he would be honored by having the Goddard Space Center named after him.

219.

1 9 4 4 — B R E T T O N   W O O D S   C O N F E R E N C E

Far from the sounds of battle, in the serene setting of Bretton
Woods, New Hampshire, a United Nations monetary and financial conference took place during the first three weeks of July
1944 that would lay the foundations for the economics of the postwar world. Finance ministers from forty-four nations agreed to a
fixed exchange rate between nations, but without a return to the
gold standard. In addition, the International Monetary Fund and
the World Bank were founded. Both of these organizations would

play a major role in restoring Europe to economic health after the war, and would be vital to world economic stability for the rest of the century. In 1998, for example, they were crucial players in dealing with the Asian economic crisis.

220.

1944—GENERAL DE GAULLE RETURNS TO PARIS

After the fall of France in 1940, Charles de Gaulle had fled to England and organized the Free French forces. A master of politics, he ingratiated himself with Churchill and later with other Allied leaders, who gave him important backing. As the Allies began to reclaim the coast of France in the summer of 1944, de Gaulle's Provisional Government of the Republic of France was given authority over liberated areas. When Paris was reclaimed, de Gaulle boldly returned to march in the August 26 victory parade, even though there were German snipers at large in the city. He then gave a radio speech in which he talked as though the French, and the French alone, had liberated the country. The other Allied leaders were not amused. They were seeing a new side of General de Gaulle, getting their first taste of a hauteur they would be coping with for another quarter-century.

221.

1944—ROOSEVELT WINS FOURTH TERM

Having broken precedent by running for a third term, there was less outcry than might be expected against Roosevelt trying for a fourth. Once again, he let himself be "drafted"; with American forces fighting around the world, the voters were less than willing to "change horses in midstream." But, with Roosevelt's behind-the-scenes approval, Henry Wallace was dumped as the candidate for vice president. In his place, Roosevelt chose Missouri Senator Harry Truman, who had impressed Roosevelt with his grasp of the need for a powerful war production board to oversee military procurement. The Republican candidate, New York Governor Thomas E. Dewey, supported most New Deal legislation and the idea of a future United Nations, which made it difficult to distinguish himself from Roosevelt. Roosevelt won by 432 electoral votes to Dewey's 99, although his popular vote declined.

222.

1945—AMERICAN FLAG RAISED AT IWO JIMA

Perhaps the single most famous photograph taken during World War II was of the American flag being raised atop Mount Suribachi on Iwo Jima on February 23, 1945. Iwo Jima was a Japanese island, only eight square miles in size, but it was of enormous strategic importance, having three airstrips and lying close enough to Japan that American fighter planes would be able to reach Toyko and return. Two flags were actually raised in the same spot on February 23, four days after the American invasion. A small one was hoisted aloft in midmorning, but then a much larger, eight-by-four-foot flag was brought from an offshore ship. The larger flag would be visible for much greater distances. Although the raising of both flags was photographed, it was the second picture that would become the model for the Marine Corps War Memorial in Arlington, Virginia. The capture of Mount Suribachi was only the start of the Iwo Jima campaign. The Japanese were so deeply dug in that it would take another month of yard-by-yard fighting to secure the island.

223.

1945—YALTA

At Yalta in the Russian Crimea, Joseph Stalin was host to Winston Churchill and President Franklin Roosevelt, beginning on February 4, 1945. Churchill was distracted by looming political problems at home, and Roosevelt, who would die in just over two months, was gravely tired. They extracted a promise from Stalin to hold free elections in Eastern Europe after the war, but did not get the details sufficiently nailed down. The repercussions of that fail-ure would last until the collapse of the Soviet Union in 1989. Stalin did keep another promise made at Yalta, however—to join the war against the Japanese once the Germans were defeated. In August 1945, the Japanese surrender would be brought about not only by the dropping of atomic bombs on Hiroshima and Nagasaki, but also by the fact that Stalin had attacked Japanese defenses in Manchuria with a million and a half men.

224.

1945—HITLER COMMITS SUICIDE

On April 29, 1945, Adolf Hitler married his longtime mistress, Eva Braun, as the Allied forces approached Berlin. In his secret Berlin bunker, the couple committed suicide the next day, and the new Führer, Admiral Karl Doenitz, surrendered a week later. Be-cause the remains of Hitler and Braun were quickly cremated, an international investigative committee was formed to establish the certainty of Hitler's death. Although his death was corroborated beyond any doubt, there would always be some people who be-lieved that Hitler had escaped to South America, as so many other German war criminals managed to do.

225.

1945—THE EUROPEAN WAR OVER

On May 8, 1945, the headline of *The New York Times* had the following first line: THE WAR IN EUROPE IS ENDED! This was the first time since the end of World War I that the *Times* had deigned to use an exclamation point in a headline, a device it usually left to the tabloid papers. The front-page picture was of the wildly jubilant crowds in Times Square celebrating the unconditional surrender of Nazi Germany. Ironically, the *Times* story carried the by-line not of one its own reporters but of Edward Kennedy, the chief of the Associated Press staff on the western front. He had sent the dispatch from Rheims, France, disobeying the orders of the Supreme Allied Command to hold the story until the next day, when the surrender was due to be announced simultaneously in Washington, London, and Moscow. Thanks to Mr. Kennedy, the world knew that the European war was over before VE-day was officially proclaimed.

226.

1945—POTSDAM CONFERENCE

From July 17 to August 7, 1945, following the surrender of Nazi Germany, but with the war in the Pacific against the Japanese still raging, President Harry Truman met with Joseph Stalin and Winston Churchill at Potsdam, a suburb of bombed-out Berlin. Stalin, as he had at Yalta six months earlier, managed to conceal many of his designs on postwar Europe. Two major side events took place. President Truman received coded assurances that the atomic bomb worked, and decided on July 24 that it would be used against Japan. On July 26, Churchill received the bitter news that he had been cast out of office by the British people. Americans found it hard to understand how the British could treat the great wartime leader so badly, but there were good reasons for the vote.

During the war, Churchill's Conservative party and Clement Atlee's Labour party had formed a coalition government. Churchill, as prime minister, was in charge of the conduct of the war, but the home front had largely been under the jurisdiction of the Labour party. Labour had instituted innumerable measures that would become the foundations of the welfare state, and the voters felt that Labour should be given the chance to consolidate its new ideas in peacetime. Churchill, however, would be elected prime minister again in 1951. During the last few days of the Potsdam Conference, Clement Atlee, as the new prime minister, joined the other three leaders in Germany.

227.

1945—ATOMIC BOMB DROPPED ON HIROSHIMA

The first atomic bomb, designed by J. Robert Oppenheimer, and built at Los Alamos, New Mexico, with a team of atomic scientists under the leadership of General Leslie R. Groves, was exploded near Alamagordo, New Mexico, on July 16, 1945. Three weeks later, by order of President Harry Truman, a bomb nicknamed "Fat Boy" was dropped on the Japanese city of Hiroshima. This August 6 event changed the world more quickly and radically than any other in history. Under a three-line banner headline on August 7, *The New York Times* carried columns describing the president's announcement of the bombing, the first descriptions of the test three weeks earlier, and an account of the three "Hidden Cities," Oak Ridge, Tennessee; Richland Village, Washington; and the still secret site in New Mexico where the bomb had been built by a hundred thousand people, most of whom hadn't "the slightest idea what they were making." The column on the president's announcement was headed NEW AGE USHERED, but the only reports from Hiroshima focused on the fact that, as the headline put it, TRAINS CANCELLED IN STRICKEN AREA. It would be some time before the world truly grasped the magnitude of what had occurred, or learned of the full horror visited upon the city of Hiroshima.

228.

1946—THE "IRON CURTAIN"

Although he was no longer prime minister of Great Britain, Winston Churchill remained an immense presence on the postwar scene. He was working on the history of the war that would bring him the Nobel Prize for Literature in 1956, and making speeches that had enormous effect. Speaking at Westminster College in Fulton, Missouri, on March 5, he coined the term "Iron Curtain," warning about Communist expansion in Europe. It was a phrase that would enter the language to describe the Eastern European countries under Soviet domination during a Cold War that would last for another four decades.

229.

1946—"SPOCK SAYS"

The postwar baby boom started with a huge leap in the American birthrate in 1946—to 3.4 million births. That same year saw the publication of Dr. Benjamin Spock's *Common Sense Book of Baby and Child Care*. It would become the bible of American child care for decades, in successive editions, and its calm advice and permissive child-rearing views would play a major role in the shaping of American society in the second half of the century. Dr. Spock would later engender controversy with his strong views against the war in Vietnam and with his conversion to vegetarianism in the 1990s, but his ideas about child care permeated the American scene. By the time Benjamin Spock died in 1998, more than fifty million copies of various editions of his baby care book had been sold around the world.

230.

1946 — NAZI WAR LEADERS CONDEMNED TO DEATH

On October 1, 1946, the Nuremberg war crimes tribunal condemned twelve Nazi war leaders to death by hanging; three others were acquitted, and another nine were given prison terms ranging from twenty years to life. The most famous of those sentenced to hang was Hermann Göring, one of Hitler's earliest followers and the founder of the notorious secret police, the Gestapo. During the first part of World War II, Göring was in charge of all German air forces, but their inability to stop the Allied air raids caused Hitler to dismiss his close lieutenant. It was because of his activities as head of the Gestapo that Göring was convicted. He committed suicide two hours before his scheduled hanging.

231.

1946 — ENIAC

The computer age got off to an extremely bulky start in 1946 with the demonstration of the Electronic Numerical Integrator and Calculator, dubbed ENIAC, at the University of Pennsylvania in Philadelphia. Built with government funding by J. Presper Eckert and John Mauchly, it was larger than a railroad boxcar. Its eighteen thousand vacuum tubes burned out at an alarming rate and had to be constantly replaced. Although it could carry out five thousand calculations a second, many switches had to be reset and some elements actually rewired in order to do different kinds of calculations. The mathematician John von Neumann suggested that the program instructions be put into the computer itself; so Mauchly and Eckert built a new machine called UNIVAC on that basis. However, it remained very large, and it was not until transistors, invented by American physicists John Bardeen, Walter H. Brattain, and William Shockley, were substituted for vacuum tubes that computers began to have real commercial possibilities. By the mid-1950s, Thomas J. Watson had bet the future of his company, IBM, on computers, and a new [era] began.

232.

1947—THE MARSHALL PLAN

George C. Marshall was the army chief of staff during World War II. He had wanted to head the forces in Europe, but President Roosevelt told him that he was too valuable, and that he was needed in Washington. General Dwight D. Eisenhower was named to the post in Europe instead, and reaped the glory of the Allied victory, but much of the strategy he implemented originated with Marshall. After President Harry Truman named Marshall secretary of state in 1947, he immediately set about organizing the European Recovery Program, which has ever since been known as the Marshall Plan. The severe economic reprisals against Germany after World War I had been partially responsible for the rise of Hitler, and the Allied countries did not want to repeat that mistake. Under Marshall's direction, the European Recovery Program dispensed more than $12 billion in aid from 1947 to 1951 to countries devastated by the war, including the defeated Germany and Italy. His leadership of this endeavor brought him the Nobel Peace Prize in 1953.

233.

1947—JACKIE ROBINSON BREAKS THE
BASEBALL COLOR LINE

A standout athlete in four sports at the University of California, Jackie Robinson was signed in 1946 by Branch Rickey of the Brooklyn Dodgers, and assigned to the team's farm club in Montreal, where he led the league in batting. Rickey was determined to break baseball's color line, but knew he had to have just the right player to do it with. Robinson had obvious superstar talent but also something else: he possessed the calm, intelligence, and personal strength needed by any man chosen to become the first black player in the major leagues. Brought up to the Brooklyn Dodgers in 1947, he met with coolness from many of his own teammates, antagonism from members of other teams, and racist taunts from far too many baseball fans. But he kept cool and stole twenty-eight bases, batted .297, and earned the first official Rookie of the Year honors. The following year, he was the National League Batting Champion and its Most Valuable Player, and would help lead the team to six World Series in his ten-year career. In the end, he became one of the great icons of twentieth-century American sports.

234.

1947—PARTITION OF INDIA AND PAKISTAN

Control of India had been transferred from the British East India Company to the British Crown in 1857, making Queen Victoria empress of India as well as queen of Great Britain. India had chafed under British rule from the end of the nineteenth century, and the National Congress Party, led by Mohandas Gandhi and Jawaharlal Nehru, demanded independence. However, because of strife between the Hindus and Muslims within the country, the first step toward independence came at the cost of dividing the country into two parts, India and Pakistan, in 1947. India became a sovereign republic in 1950, and Pakistan in 1956, but there has been hostility between the two ever since partition. The enmity between the two countries continues to be such that when India tested atomic bombs in 1998, Pakistan immediately followed suit.

235.

1947—BREAKING THE SOUND BARRIER

We are now completely used to the sonic boom that results when a jet breaks the sound barrier, but it was noise that had never been heard before on October 14, 1947. On that date, Captain Charles "Chuck" Yeager, twenty-four, was dropped from a B-29 at the controls of a "rocket plane" called the X-1. Although rigorous ground tests had been made, no one was certain that the X-1's fuel tanks would not explode when Yeager started the engines at forty thousand feet. Yeager himself had managed to conceal from his superiors that he had broken two ribs in a riding accident two days earlier, impeding the use of his right arm.

The test was a success as Yeager flew at more than 700 mph above the New Mexico desert. It would be years before such speeds could be achieved by planes that took off from the ground, but on that day in 1947, Yeager demonstrated the "right stuff" that would make him the mentor to the first generation of American astronauts fifteen years later.

236.

1947—POLAROID CAMERA

As a student at Harvard, Edwin Herbert Land began experimenting with polarized light, and had patented his first invention, a material used to eliminate glare, by the time he was twenty-three, in 1932. Fifteen years later, after securing numerous other patents, he produced his revolutionary Polaroid Land Camera, which provided a finished photograph one minute after the shutter was snapped. Polaroid cameras really took off in sales, however, when Land perfected color Polaroid film in 1962. His company spent years in court fighting the production of copycat cameras by other companies. His invention remains a unique contribution to modern photography, used for family snapshots, employed by innumerable businesses, and integral to the work of many modern artists.

237.

1948—GANDHI ASSASSINATED

On January 30, 1948, Mohandas K. Gandhi, known as Mahatma (Great Teacher), was killed with a bullet fired while walking to the pergola where he was to deliver his daily prayer message. As a politician, and especially as a spiritual leader, Gandhi was regarded as the father of modern India. He began working to bring about the independence of India from Great Britain in 1915, giving up Western ways, even though he was a distinguished lawyer, and took up an ascetic life. Preaching not only his own Hindu ethics, but also Christian and Muslim ideas, he asserted the unity of humanity under one God. An advocate of passive resistance to Great Britain, he was nevertheless arrested several times, but was always released because of the vastness of his following in India—the British could not afford to make him a martyr. Although Gandhi was a leader in bringing about independence in 1947, he was against the partition of India and Pakistan, and preached reconciliation between Hindus and Muslims. He was murdered by a Hindu fanatic who opposed any overtures to Muslims. Gandhi's belief in passive resistance had a great influence around the world, and was a direct inspiration for the Reverend Martin Luther King, Jr.'s leadership of the American civil rights movement.

238.

1948—THE STATE OF ISRAEL IS BORN

With the termination of the British Mandate governing Palestine at midnight on May 15, 1948, the State of Israel came into being with a proclamation by David Ben-Gurion, chairman of the National Council and the new country's first premier. Under the threat of an Egyptian invasion, the new country was cheered by its immediate recognition by the United States as a sovereign state. Washington had been against the Jewish National Council moving so quickly to declare sovereignty, but once the declaration was made, President Harry Truman moved with great speed to acknowledge the de facto authority of Israel. The American statement was coupled with an expression of hope for peace in Palestine—establishing from the first moment America's role as a broker for peace that would continue for the rest of the century.

239.

1948—APARTHEID FORMALIZED

Although the white minority in South Africa, of English and Dutch origin, had ruled the black majority with an iron hand for more than 250 years, the platform of the Afrikaner Nationalist party, the most authoritarian of the white leadership coalitions, called for a policy of "apartheid" in 1948, which was instituted by degrees over the next several years. It divided the population of the country into four groups: Whites, Coloureds (of mixed race), Asiatics, and Bantu (the name for the native population, which accounted for 70 percent of the whole). The Bantus were further subdivided into two groups, a ploy that had the blacks in opposition to one another until the 1990s. None of these groups was to have any social or sexual contact with the other. Rigid separation by locale was enforced, and those who did work in other areas had to carry documentation at all times.

240.

1948—''DEWEY DEFEATS TRUMAN''

In one of the most embarrassing mistakes by a newspaper in the twentieth century, the early edition of the *Chicago Tribune* the day after the 1948 presidential election carried a banner headline declaring Republican nominee Thomas Dewey, who had been defeated by Franklin Delano Roosevelt in 1944, the victor on his second try. That led to one of the famous political photographs of the century as a grinning Harry Truman held the errant paper aloft.

The *Tribune* had misread the early returns and put too much faith in polls showing Truman being defeated by at least five percentage points. The pollsters excused themselves by pointing out that they had stopped polling five days before the election, and they promised to poll right up until election day in the future. They kept that promise, but it should be noted that even with last-minute polling, they miscalled the 1996 presidential election by an even bigger margin. They had the right winner, Bill Clinton, so not that much attention was paid to their error, but all the major polls had President Clinton defeating Senator Robert Dole by sixteen points the evening before the election. The difference was only eight points, a bigger spread than in 1948, which may suggest that even today the polls are not as reliable as their practitioners and the press would have people believe.

241.

1948—THE LONG-PLAYING RECORD

Peter Goldmark was born in Hungary, trained in Vienna, and emigrated to the United States in 1933, where he went to work in the laboratories of the Columbia Broadcasting System. Goldmark was one of the foremost figures in the development of modern sound and visual transmission. He was the primary genius behind the development of the long-playing (LP) 33⅓-rpm record, introduced in 1948. The light vinyl disk, with its forty-minute-plus playing time and improved sound, completely replaced the old 78-rpm record. With the advent of CDs (compact disks) in the 1980s, it looked as though the LP might also become a dinosaur. However, by the late 1990s it started to climb again in popularity, due to what many music lovers consider a warmer sound than CDs, and because its large format covers have retained their appeal.

Peter Goldmark also designed the first practical color television system, used on an experimental basis in 1940, and later developed special satellite cameras for NASA.

242.

1949—THE PEOPLE'S REPUBLIC OF CHINA

In the renewed conflict between the Chinese Communists and Nationalists that began in 1945, after the defeat of Japan, one major city after another fell to the Communists. On October 1, 1949, the People's Republic of China was proclaimed under the leadership of Mao Tse-tung. The defeated General Chiang Kai-shek fled to Taiwan, where he established the Nationalist Republic of China, which was recognized and supported by the United States. The problem of the "two Chinas" would vex American foreign policy for the remainder of the century. American political beliefs demanded that the United States support Nationalist China, with its more democratic processes, but it was impossible to ignore the size and power of the People's Republic.

243.

1949—RADIOCARBON DATING

Since the 1930s, scientists had been aware that the carbon inherent in all living things on earth underwent a gradual process of radioactive decay following the demise of any given organism. But in 1949, chemist Walter Libby published a practical formula for measuring the rate of the decay. The formula made it possible for archeologists to arrive at dates, accurate within two hundred years, of fossils that were thousands—or millions—of years old. There was some initial resistance to carbon dating because it showed how far off the "guesswork" of many prominent scientists had been in terms of dating fossils. The new method prevailed, however, and led to sweeping revisions about numerous events, including when the dinosaurs actually lived to when humans first crossed the Bering Strait from Asia to the North American continent. Radiocarbon dating has vastly increased our understanding of the earth's history and of our own place in it.

244.

1949—NATIONAL BASKETBALL ASSOCIATION

In 1891, Dr. James Naismith invented basketball at a YMCA in Springfield, Massachusetts. It caught on quickly, not just in the United States but around the world, and was first included in the Olympic Games in 1936. There had been professional teams in the United States from early in the twentieth century, but it was with the formation of the NBA in 1949 that basketball moved up to rank with baseball and football as the "Big 3" of American sports. It is now a major professional sport around the world, with top players from other countries signing with the NBA and secondary players from the United States making large salaries abroad. Basketball has become the major sports development of the century, with huge economic and cultural effects.

245.

1950—FIRST ORGAN TRANSPLANT

The patient was named Ruth Tucker, and she was forty-nine years old. On June 17, 1950, at the Little Company of Mary Hospital in Chicago, Illinois, head surgeon Dr. Richard H. Lawler removed Tucker's malfunctioning kidney and replaced it with one from a donor of the same blood type and age who had died only minutes before of a long-term condition that had not affected kidney function. Ruth Tucker would live for another five years, and her death was from causes unrelated to her kidney transplant. A new age had begun in medicine, one that would lead to transplants of most of the major internal organs. Kidney transplants have become routine.

246.

1950—THE KOREAN WAR BEGINS

The Korean civil war between the Communist North and the South Korean Republic became an international conflict in June 1950 when North Korea launched a full-scale invasion of South Korea. On June 29, President Harry Truman, with the backing of the United Nations Security Council, ordered United States air and naval forces to assist the government of South Korea in repulsing the invasion, and enforcing an earlier cease-fire arranged by the United Nations. By July 1, sixteen UN member nations had sent troops to Korea, but most of the forces there were American, and at the urging of the UN, Truman appointed an American Supreme Commander, for all forces, naming General Douglas MacArthur. Less than five years after the surrender of Japan, America was fighting a new war in the Pacific.

247.

1950—THE DINER'S CLUB CARD

In 1950, the Diner's Club issued the first modern credit card. While many department stores had introduced credit cards earlier, the Diner's Club card was the first that could be used at many different locations both nationally and internationally. Competitors soon followed suit, including American Express, banks began issuing their own credit cards, and then turned to cards issued by the two giants in the field, Visa and MasterCard. The use of credit cards greatly increased in the 1960s, and soon became a virtual necessity to travelers wishing to make advance reservations for hotel rooms or rental cars. As computer technology made striking advances in the 1980s, and with the introduction of automatic teller machines (ATMs), credit cards became not only ubiquitous, but held out the promise of a world in which electronic money would eventually all but replace cash, although many experts feel that this development is not as imminent as some enthusiasts suggest. Credit cards have also had a vast effect on the consumer economy, including a serious downside in terms of the rise of consumer debt. While the credit card is one of the most important economic developments of the twentieth century, the term itself was actually coined in 1888 by Edward Bellamy in his hugely popular novel *Looking Backward*, set in Boston, Massachusetts, in the year 2000.

248.

1950—ALGER HISS CONVICTED

A United States State Department official, who rose to become the coordinator of all U.S. foreign policy, Alger Hiss was accused in 1948 of helping to transmit confidential documents to the

Soviet Union. His chief accuser was Whittaker Chambers, an editor who confessed to being a Communist courier. In the second of two trials, Hiss was convicted of perjury and sentenced to five years in prison, but was released after four. A congressional investigation of Hiss brought to prominence a young California congressman named Richard M. Nixon, who would later be elected U.S. senator on the basis of his anti-Communist credentials and then be chosen as Dwight D. Eisenhower's vice-presidential running mate in 1952. Hiss always maintained his innocence, and there were many who believed him. He remained highly controversial and the subject of intermittent public debate for another forty-five years. Even his death in 1997 at the age of ninety-three did not end the argument.

249.

1951—TRUMAN FIRES MACARTHUR

In April 1951, General Douglas MacArthur, the Supreme Commander of the United States and United Nations forces in Korea, openly challenged the Truman/UN policy on the conduct of the war in a letter to the Republican minority leader of the House of Representatives, Joseph Martin of Massachusetts. MacArthur wanted to open a second front on mainland China, challenging Communist rule, and bring the troops of General Chiang Kai-shek, who was defeated by the Communists in 1949, back into the fray. Not only would this have meant a much wider war, but MacArthur's open defiance was something no American president and commander in chief could tolerate. Truman took a great political risk in firing the popular World War II hero, but although MacArthur was welcomed by vast throngs on his return to America, the country as a whole was in no mood for a larger war, and MacArthur's prestige soon waned. The Korean War, however, would drag on for another two years. One of General Dwight D. Eisenhower's campaign pledges as the Republican candidate for president in 1952 was that he would personally go to Korea to help find a settlement. On July 27, 1953, four months after Eisenhower became president, an armistice was signed dividing Korea into two nations at the 38th parallel. United States troops, under United Nations auspices, have remained to guard the border ever since.

250.

1952—DICK BUTTON'S TRIPLE JUMP

At the 1952 Olympics at Oslo, Norway, Dick Button of the United States performed the first triple jump, a triple loop, in the history of competitive figure skating, winning his second Olympic gold medal. In the course of his amateur career, Button also won seven U.S. Championships and five World Championships. He had also invented the flying camel, a move used by all top skaters to this day. By demonstrating that a triple jump was physically possible, he changed the sport of figure skating forever. Later skaters added many other triple jumps, and starting in the 1990s, even began to land quadruple jumps in competition. It was Dick Button who showed the way.

251.

1952—DWIGHT EISENHOWER ELECTED
PRESIDENT

Although the Democratic candidate for president, Illinois Governor Adlai E. Stevenson III, gave brilliant, substantive speeches, he didn't stand a chance against World War II hero Dwight David Eisenhower. "I Like Ike" was the Republican campaign slogan, and the country did. The biggest controversy during the campaign concerned accusations that Eisenhower's running mate, Senator Richard M. Nixon, had been the beneficiary of a slush fund, and Eisenhower was prepared to kick him off the ticket. However, he allowed Nixon to make a speech to the country on television. "The Checkers Speech," as it came to be known because Nixon said the only gift he'd ever taken was the family dog Checkers, saved Nixon's career, and the Eisenhower-Nixon ticket won in a landslide 442 electoral votes to Stevenson's 89. Stevenson's grandfather, the first Adlai, had been Grover Cleveland's second vice president, but that kind of pedigree didn't count against Ike.

252.

1952—HYDROGEN BOMB

The explosive force of an atomic bomb is caused by nuclear fission. A hydrogen bomb creates an even greater explosion through a fusion process in which lighter elements are "fused" to form heavier elements. Because the result of the fusion is actually lighter than the total weight of the compounds that went into it, the remaining mass is expelled as energy of devastating strength. The heat required to create this fusion makes it necessary to use an atom bomb as a trigger to set off the hydrogen bomb, which is therefore also called a "thermonuclear bomb."

The first hydrogen bomb was exploded in a test by the United States at Eniwetok Atoll in the Marshall Islands, a U.S. protectorate in the Pacific Ocean, in November 1952. The bomb had an explosive power equivalent to ten million tons of TNT, but much larger bombs were subsequently built. The Soviet Union had acquired its own hydrogen bomb by the following year, and the nuclear arsenals of both the United States and the Soviet Union would eventually consist primarily of hydrogen bombs.

253.

1 9 5 3 — D N A

DNA is short for deoxyribonucleic acid, the principal constituent of the chromosomes that determine our heredity. James Dewey Watson of the United States and Francis Crick of Great Britain announced in 1953 that they had uncovered the "double helix" structure of this complex nucleic acid, and they shared the 1968 Nobel Prize in Physiology or Medicine for their pioneering work.

Since our DNA is as unique as our fingerprints, the ability to run DNA tests from blood samples has made it possible to ascertain the paternity of a child in contested legitimacy cases. DNA testing can be used in criminal cases, if the perpetrator has left any trace of bodily fluid, hair, or even particles of skin from a scratch that remain under the fingernails of a victim, to identify the perpetrator or rule out a suspect. It took thirty-five years for DNA tests to become foolproof to the extent that courts would accept them; but now a number of imprisoned individuals have had their convictions overturned on the basis of surviving DNA evidence from the crime scene.

Because the DNA of even many ancient fossils can be determined, this testing has become an invaluable tool in archeological research. The identification of DNA is also crucial to the field of molecular biology, including the ability to clone organisms. It is thus a key element in what many believe will be the most important scientific field in the twenty-first century as gene manipulation and gene splicing become common, making possible the alteration of heredity.

254.

1953—EVEREST CONQUERED

Mount Everest, the world's highest mountain, located in the Himalayas, rises 29,028 feet, and had resisted all attempts to reach its peak until 1953. It was finally conquered by Edmund Hillary of Australia and his Sherpa guide, Tenzing Norkay, on May 29, 1953. Everest has been successfully climbed many times since, but it has also been the scene of numerous climbing tragedies. The news that a British flag was now flying atop Mount Everest reached Queen Elizabeth II just hours before she left Buckingham Palace for her coronation. Hillary was knighted shortly thereafter.

255.

1953—CORONATION OF ELIZABETH II

The coronation of Elizabeth II, then twenty-six years old, at Westminster Abbey on June 2, 1953, was the first such ceremony to be televised, and it attracted millions of viewers around the world. These scenes of royal pageantry, staged with a grandeur and finesse that no other country can rival on state occasions, served to increase tourist travel to England and to bring an outpouring of affection for the young queen. For all the troubles that have been visited on the royal family in recent years, millions of people remember that day in 1953 as one of the great spectacles of the century.

256.

1953—SUCCESSFUL IMPREGNATION WITH
FROZEN SPERM

In 1953, a team of doctors at the University of Iowa Medical School was the first to succeed at using frozen male sperm to impregnate a woman. By the 1980s, such procedures were becoming relatively commonplace, and sperm banks had been established in most major American cities and at medical schools across the country. Sperm banks initially made use of carefully screened anonymous donors, but also became repositories for the sperm of men who had undergone vasectomies for birth control purposes but wished to retain the option of fathering a child by artificial insemination at a later date. The possibility of using frozen sperm to achieve pregnancy has made it possible for large numbers of women to have children, but in recent years has also given rise to lawsuits in some cases when a couple divorced or the donor husband died. The courts have decided these cases in favor of the donors, who either did not want the sperm used after a divorce or who forbade its use in a will.

257.

1954—NUCLEAR-POWERED SUBMARINE

Named the *Nautilus* in honor of Captain Nemo's submarine in Jules Verne's *Twenty-Thousand Leagues Under the Sea*, the world's first nuclear-powered submarine was launched by the United States Navy on January 21, 1954. Because of their ability to remain submerged for almost unlimited periods of time, nuclear submarines became one of the most potent weapons during the Cold War. Equipped with nuclear missiles by both the United States and the Soviet Union, these vessels could be expected to survive any nuclear-bomb attack on land masses, and thus served as a restraining element in the "balance of terror" between the free world and the Communist powers.

258.

1954—BREAKING THE FOUR-MINUTE MILE

At the Iffley Road Sports Ground in Oxford, England, on May 6, 1954, twenty-five-year-old British runner Roger Bannister became the first man to run a mile in under four minutes. It had long been considered impossible to break the four-minute barrier, but Bannister was clocked in 3 minutes, 59.4 seconds. Many runners have been clocked under four minutes since, but the difficulty of Bannister's task can be measured by the fact that no one has been able to take more than another ten seconds off his record. Bannister was knighted in 1975.

259.

1954—POLIO VACCINE

Poliomyelitis, also called infantile paralysis or simply polio, was one of the most feared childhood diseases until the mid-1950s. In its severe form, the virus could paralyze its victims, or even lead to death because it often prevented the lungs from functioning properly. While children were its main victims, it sometimes struck adults as well; Franklin Delano Roosevelt's legs were crippled by the disease, as dramatized in the Broadway play and Hollywood movie *Sunrise at Campobello*.

Jonas Edward Salk, a microbiologist at the University of Pittsburgh, developed a killed-virus vaccine, administered by injection, that was successfully tested on public school children in Pittsburgh in 1954. Dr. Albert Bruce Sabin, who was born in Russia but emigrated to the United States in 1921, developed a live-virus vaccine that was taken orally. It went into use in 1959. The work of these two men succeeded in virtually eradicating polio from the advanced nations of the world, and its incidence has been drastically reduced even in the poorest countries.

260.

1954—CIGARETTES CAUSE CANCER

The antismoking drive that has reached a crescendo in the United States in the late 1990s had its start with a report by the National Cancer Institute in 1954 that there was a link between smoking and cancer. Subsequently, hundreds of other studies led to increasingly strong health warnings being carried by law on cigarette packs, the banning of cigarette advertising from television, lawsuits against cigarette companies by cancer victims, and government charges at both the state and local level that the tobacco companies have consistently lied about their awareness of the dangers of their products.

While few people try to argue that smoking is anything but bad for the health, there are those who point out that combustion engines, even with their new environmental controls, are even worse, but that nobody talks about banning them. The loss of civility between smokers and nonsmokers has at times become seriously dismaying to cultural observers. In the course of the twentieth century smoking has gone from being shocking, when practiced by women in the first two decades of the century, to the epitome of sophistication, to being looked upon as something worse than a vice and closer to a sin. And the latter phase had its beginnings in the National Cancer Institute report in 1954.

261.

1954—SOLAR BATTERIES

The Bell Telephone Laboratories announced the development of a new kind of battery in 1954, one that was powered simply by converting sunlight—or strong electric light—to energy. Solar batteries were initially more of a novelty item than anything else, but they led to developments that could be extremely important in the twenty-first century. By the 1970s, large solar panels had been developed that could be placed on the roofs of buildings in sunny areas to cut electricity bills considerably, and in some advanced models, to replace regular electricity completely. Income-tax credits were voted by some states, including California, and by the U.S. Congress to encourage the use of solar panels in the wake of the oil crises of the 1970s. However, these laws did not sit well with power and energy providers, and they were rescinded under President Ronald Reagan by Congress, and simultaneously in California under Republican Governor George Deukmejian, both of whom were keeping campaign promises to do so. In 1948, solar power was a $415 million industry; but without the tax credits it virtually collapsed, taking in only $20 million in 1986. There are nevertheless many experts who believe that solar power is still a wave of the future, and both environmental groups and the politicians who back them are still working to that end.

262.

1954—NORTHLAND SHOPPING MALL

The first "strip mall" shopping center, with several stores ranged in a line behind a joint parking lot, was built at the end of the nineteenth century in Maryland, even before the advent of the automobile. As cars became common, more and larger such shopping centers were built around the country. It was not until 1954, however, that the first modern shopping mall, with major department stores and an internal pedestrian walkway, lined with stores opening onto it, was built. It was the Northland Shopping Mall in the suburbs of Detroit. Since that time, shopping malls have become the most popular destinations for American consumers outside the major cities. They have added to suburban sprawl and road congestion, and have often had a profoundly damaging economic effect on the centers of small and large cities. Very few environmentalists, city planners, or architectural critics have a good word to say about shopping malls, and many people profess to hate them, but they remain one of the most important consumer innovations of the second half of the century.

263.

1954 — MCCARTHYISM

The word "McCarthyism" was coined by the great political cartoonist Herblock (Herbert Lawrence Block), then in his forties, to describe the witchhunt perpetrated by Senator Joseph R. McCarthy of Wisconsin, a master of accusation and innuendo who took it as his personal duty to rout out the American Communists he believed to be everywhere, even infesting the State Department and other branches of government. Aided by the House Un-American Activities Committee, which specialized in routing out Communists in show business, ruining the careers of former party members (there had been a great many of these in the 1930s, before Stalin's butchery disillusioned them) and of so-called sympathizers, McCarthy and his cohorts unleased a 1,700-day reign of terror in the United States. Even President Eisenhower was afraid of McCarthy, a Republican like himself, and did not even defend his friend and mentor George C. Marshall, the Army Chief of Staff during World War II, when he was attacked. Then McCarthy took a wrong step, and decided to go after supposed Communists in the U.S. Army. The Army-McCarthy hearings were televised, and the nation watched them intently for thirty days. On the thirtieth day, the private attorney hired by the Army, Joseph Welch, finally had had enough. When McCarthy attacked a young lawyer from Welch's own firm in a vicious, lengthy tirade, Welch said, "Let us not assassinate this lad further, Senator. You have done enough. Have you no sense of decency, sir, at long last? Have you left no sense of decency?" The hearing room broke into applause, and the reign of terror was effectively over. On December 2, the Senate would censure their own member by a vote of sixty-seven to twenty-two.

264.

1955 — ROSA PARKS AND THE MONTGOMERY BUS BOYCOTT

In 1955, the Interstate Commerce Commission ordered an end to segregation on long-distance buses, but in the South, local buses were still segregated. In Montgomery, Alabama, a black woman named Rosa Parks boarded a nearly empty bus and refused an order to move to the rear of the vehicle, continuing to sit at the front in the area reserved for whites. Seldom has such a simple act of courage by an ordinary person had such repercussions. Rosa Parks was arrested and taken off the bus. When news of what had happened to her spread, a boycott of the Montgomery buses by black citizens, led by the Reverend Dr. Martin Luther King, Jr., was organized. The boycott, and the demands for an end to segregation, went on for nearly a year, from December 1, 1955, to November of the next year. The boycott came to an end with the United States Supreme Court decision of November, 13, 1956, that ruled the segregation of buses unconstitutional. Rosa Parks became an icon of the American civil rights movement, an honor she accepted with quiet, modest dignity.

265.

1956—THE HUNGARIAN UPRISING

Demonstrations by students in Budapest called for a democratic government and the return of Premier Imre Nagy, who although a Communist had loosened government controls during his tenure, beginning in 1953. He had been removed in 1955 and a Soviet stooge named Erno Gero had been appointed premier. The uprising spread and turned violent, with one student commandeering a tank and using it to pull over a massive statue of Stalin. Nagy was brought back, formed a new government that included non-Communists, and as the students had demanded, released Cardinal Mindszenty, who had been imprisoned for eight years. Soviet troops then invaded Hungary, and Nagy was arrested and executed in 1958. During the unsettled period from October 23 to the arrival of the Soviet troops on November 4, large numbers of Hungarian students and dissidents managed to escape to the West.

266.

1956—EISENHOWER REELECTED

The 1956 election was a repeat of 1952, as the Democrats again nominated Adlai Stevenson. Because of a heart attack, President Eisenhower's health was an issue (with the suggestion that people might really be voting for Nixon), but the voters ignored that, and Ike won an even bigger victory than the first time, 457 electoral votes to 73. His great rival, Stevenson, would try one last time for the presidency in 1960, but the nomination would go to the much younger John F. Kennedy, who would appoint Stevenson ambassador to the United Nations, a position in which Stevenson was serving when he died of a heart attack in London in 1965. Many historians regard Eisenhower and Stevenson as the most accomplished figures of their respective parties in the second half of the century, and their two contests for the presidency as offering one of the more distinguished choices in American history.

267.

1956—TELEVISION REMOTE CONTROL

The TV remote control was invented in 1956 by Dr. Robert Adler, although it did not become a standard accessory for new television sets until 1982. Dr. Adler is more amused than offended by accusations that he is responsible for the creation of "the couch potato," but his invention has had larger repercussions. Because it is so easy to change channels, many people have become "zappers," who change channels constantly to see if there is something more interesting available. Studies have shown that most zappers are men, and that this has caused tensions in many marriages. Moreover, as television critics and sociologists have noted, the ease of zapping has tended to make television programming more sensationalistic and to alter the content of news programs, with shorter and catchier segments replacing extended news reporting of major issues. Thus the remote control is a prime example of a modest technological development that has more far-reaching consequences than its inventor ever imagined.

268.

1957—CIVIL RIGHTS ACT

The first Civil Rights Act since the Reconstruction period after the Civil War was making its way through the United States Congress in the summer of 1957. It was a mild measure, but was met by fierce resistance from many southern members of Congress. Senator J. Strom Thurmond of North Carolina, in a last-ditch effort to stop the act from passage, embarked on the longest Senate filibuster in American history, talking nonstop for twenty-five hours and twenty-seven minutes on August 30. Despite this, the bill eventually cleared Congress on September 9. It was a first step toward the far more sweeping civil rights measures that would be passed under President Lyndon Johnson in the mid-1960s.

269.

1959—HAWAII BECOMES FIFTIETH STATE

On June 30, 1958, the United States Congress had admitted Alaska to the Union as the forty-ninth state. Hawaii became the fiftieth on March 12, 1959, less than a year later. The admission of these two new states, neither attached to the "lower forty-eight," within less than a year was a fresh example of the political tradeoffs that had marked the admission of several other states, particularly in the nineteenth century. For example, in the Missouri Compromise of 1820–1821, Missouri had been admitted as a slave state, while Maine was admitted as a free state. In the case of Alaska and Hawaii, the deal recognized the fact that Alaska would inevitably be a largely Republican state and Hawaii a largely Democratic one in terms of known voting patterns. Thus, to assure admission of Alaska, Republicans agreed to support the subsequent admission of Hawaii, and vice-versa.

270.

1959—CASTRO'S CUBA

Fidel Castro had begun his revolutionary activities in Cuba in 1953, when he unsuccessfully attacked an army post. After two years in prison, he went to Mexico and organized a movement called "The Twenty-sixth of July." Returning to Cuba, he, his brother Raul, Ernesto "Che" Guevara, and nine other revolutionaries set up a hidden headquarters in the Sierra Maestra mountains. Attracting considerable numbers of followers, Castro finally succeeded in ousting the corrupt dictatorship of Fulgencio Batista on January 1, 1959, and became premier of the country two days later.

His rule would survive longer than that of any other Communist leader of the century; he was still in power at the century's end, overcoming every attempt to dislodge him and a host of international crises.

271.

1959—DE GAULLE AND THE FIFTH REPUBLIC

As the leader of the French government in exile during World War II, Charles de Gaulle was easily elected provisional president of France in 1945, but resigned the following year when it became obvious that the new constitution for the Fourth Republic would have a weak executive. From 1947 to 1953, he led an opposition party he created and then retired. But in 1958, the civil war in Algeria, which was controlled by France, led to widespread unrest at home. To deal with the crisis, de Gaulle was made premier with the power to rule by decree for six months. A new constitution was created for a Fifth Republic, and de Gaulle became its powerful new president. His power, nonetheless was still not commensurate with his desires, and he resigned in 1969 after being defeated on issues of constitutional reform. He died a year later at the age of eighty. One of the most imposing, and self-important, politicians of the century, Charles de Gaulle's ten-year rule from 1959 to 1969 created many disagreements with the United States, Great Britain, and Germany, but brought France a new prestige and power in the postwar world.

272.

1960—LASERS

The word "laser" is actually an acronym for *Light Amplification by Stimulated Emission of Radiation*. The American physicist Theodore H. Maiman demonstrated the first laser in 1960, although it was established by a twenty-year patent suit that some of the underlying elements of his invention had been previously patented by another inventor, Gordon Gould.

Lasers function through the excitation of atoms so that they emit photons (a form of energy) that in turn produce an intense beam of light in a reactive process. It's not the energy level itself, however, that counts in the process; it's the narrowness of the beam, and the intensity that results from that narrowness. Lasers are powerful enough to cut through steel and can be used with the precision necessary for delicate eye operations. The potential uses of lasers have only begun to be explored, and their further development is likely to be one of the most important scientific stories of the twenty-first century. The reasons why lasers work, however, is something that a great many people who use them don't like to think about too much. They are one of the (so far) few practical applications of quantum physics, which deals in a subatomic world so bizarre that it outdoes the wildest science fiction and that gave even Albert Einstein the willies.

273.

1960—THE GUGGENHEIM MUSEUM

Frank Lloyd Wright died in 1959 as his most famous building was nearing completion. One of the most influential and famous architects of the twentieth century was born in 1869 in Richland Center, Wisconsin. A radical innovator from the start, he changed the rules of both structural elements and aesthetics. He did not like interior walls, and his removal of room divisions to create an open, fluid space had enormous impact on architects all over the world. From the Larkin Building in Buffalo, New York (1904), to Tokyo's Imperial Hotel (1923), his buildings attracted great attention. Wright's own home, "Taliesin," in Wisconsin, which was initially built in 1911 but twice reconstructed as his ideas changed, and the 1937 Kaufmann house, "Falling Water," at Bear Run, Pennsylvania, both emphasized architectural adaptation to the existing landscape. His last and most famous building, the Guggenheim Museum on Upper Fifth Avenue in New York City, took the opposite tack, standing in stark, bold contrast to the conservative buildings around it. Compared by detractors to an overgrown snail or a cement mixer, it was greeted by most critics as a masterpiece. Housing a collection of modern art, its circular, gently sloping galleries around the sides of a large, open atrium in the center sometimes caused problems in displaying art, but no visitor to this remarkable building has ever forgotten the experience.

274.

1960—FIRST TELEVISED PRESIDENTIAL DEBATES

On Monday, September 26, 1960, the first televised debate of presidential candidates in American history took place between Senator John F. Kennedy, the Democratic nominee, and Vice President Richard M. Nixon. Both the press and Nixon himself thought the vice president had the advantage, recalling his famous "Checkers" speech on television defending himself against charges of financial impropriety in 1952, and his celebrated "kitchen debate" with Soviet Premier Nikita Khrushchev at the American National Exhibition in Moscow. But the result was to reaffirm the extent to which television was a *visual* medium.

Most voters who heard the debate on the radio rated it a toss-up or a Nixon victory, and substantively Nixon certainly held his own. But on television, Kennedy looked much better. Nixon had lost weight while spending two weeks in the hospital recovering from a serious knee infection, and he was also getting over a cold. He had refused television makeup, because Kennedy had opted for it, and tried to hide his well-known five o'clock shadow with a pancake product that made him look pasty. Kennedy looked tanned and fit by contrast—it would not be until after Kennedy's death that the public would learn his health was far more fragile than Nixon's. What's more, simply by holding his own against the formidable vice president, young Senator Kennedy increased his stature.

Although Nixon would do better in three later debates, millions of Americans made up their minds that first night, and Kennedy would prove victorious. For the rest of the century, presidential debates would play a crucial part in every election.

275.

1960—JOHN F. KENNEDY ELECTED PRESIDENT

In one of the closest elections in American history, Democratic candidate Senator John F. Kennedy defeated Vice President Richard M. Nixon for the presidency. Although Kennedy won 303 electoral votes to Nixon's 219, the election was much closer than those figures would suggest. Out of 68,828,960 votes cast, Kennedy's popular margin was only 143,673, or about one vote per precinct across the country. It was later revealed that Nixon had wakened President Eisenhower at the White House with a telephone call in the middle of the night, saying that the election had been stolen with ballot-box stuffing in Chicago and in Texas. Eisenhower replied that that might be true, but that to contest the election would throw the country into a constitutional crisis. He urged Nixon to go back to bed.

276.

1961—THE "MILITARY-INDUSTRIAL COMPLEX"

In his farewell address to the American people, three days before the end of his second term as president, Dwight D. Eisenhower made what many regard as the finest and most important speech of his career. He spoke of the need to pursue mutual disarmament between the United States and the Soviet Union. He then issued a warning, and it was not to the Soviets. "[The] conjunction of an immense military establishment and a large arms industry is new in the American experience. . . . We recognize the imperative need for this development. Yet we must not fail to comprehend its grave implications. . . . In the councils of government we must guard against the acquisition of unwarranted influence, whether sought or unsought, by the military-industrial complex."

These words from the most successful and most popular American soldier-statesman of the century were duly noted as wise indeed, and then thoroughly ignored as the arms race not only continued but accelerated for another three decades. The Pentagon and industry leaders worked hand in glove to see that it did, aided by members of Congress looking to keep the plants and bases in their own states running on a full tank, not of gas, but of billions upon billions of dollars.

277.

1961—YURI GAGARIN IS FIRST MAN
TO ORBIT EARTH

On April 12, 1961, the Soviet Union announced that it had put a man into orbit around the earth. The first news came from a radio broadcast, which said: "Russia has successfully launched a man into space. His name is Yuri Gagarin. He was launched in a sputnik named Vostok, which means 'East.'" Major Gagarin orbited the earth once, attaining a height of 187 miles, and sent messages back from space. The landing, it was soon discovered, took place on land and not at sea, as the United States was planning for its own space flights. Although with Gagarin's flight the Soviet Union was able to claim a major victory in the early space race, the difficulties inherent in a "hard" landing rather than a sea landing would later prove costly to the Soviet space program.

278.

1961—RUDOLF NUREYEV DEFECTS

Leaping over barriers at Le Bourget airport in Paris, the Russian ballet dancer Rudolf Nureyev of the Kirov Ballet defected to the West on June 16, 1961, at the age of twenty-three. Finding a home at Great Britain's Royal Ballet and a new partner in the much older Dame Margot Fonteyn, Nureyev's electrifying jumps and enormous charisma gave classical ballet a new lease on life over the next twenty-five years. Despite the difference in their ages (she was born in 1919, he in 1938), Fonteyn and Nureyev formed a legendary partnership, and after she retired he went on to appear with many major companies and to stage as well as star in numerous productions of major classical works. Although other Soviet defectors such as Mikhail Baryshnikov and Natalia Makarova also made headlines and drew huge audiences, Nureyev is given the greatest credit for expanding the audience for classical ballet in the last four decades of the century.

279.

1961 — THE BERLIN WALL RISES

The political division between democratic West Berlin and Communist East Berlin became a solid physical barrier in August 1961. The famed Brandenburg Gate between the two halves of the city was closed by the East German government on August 13, and on the seventeenth and eighteenth, East German workers constructed the Berlin Wall. This almost impregnable barrier brought to a halt the stream of East Germans escaping to the West. The Berlin Wall became one of the most storied symbols of the Cold War. In June 1963, President John F. Kennedy toured West Germany, and on a visit to West Berlin he addressed a crowd of 150,000 on a platform erected in front of the Wall, saying, "All free men . . . are citizens of Berlin. And therefore, as a free man, I take pride in the words *'Ich bin ein Berliner* ['I am a Berliner'].' "

280.

1961 — THE PEACE CORPS

President John F. Kennedy created the Peace Corps in 1961. Approved and funded by Congress, it was an agency whose purpose was to assist developing countries to train people in fields suited to a country's particular needs. Thousands of Americans were sent abroad to carry out his mission. The volunteers, who had to pass rigorous physical and mental tests to be accepted, ranged from idealistic young people just out of college to quite elderly persons with talent and expertise. Among the older volunteers was Lillian Carter, mother of President Jimmy Carter, who served in India.

281.

1962—JOHN GLENN IS FIRST AMERICAN
TO ORBIT EARTH

The U.S. space program caught up with the efforts of the Soviet Union in 1962, when Colonel John Glenn became the first American to orbit the earth. His three orbits of the earth also surpassed the effort of Yuri Gagarin, the Russian who had completed one orbit in 1961. In May 1961 between these two orbital flights, the United States had launched Commander Alan B. Shepard, Jr., 115 miles into space, and Shepard landed in the Atlantic 15 minutes later. John Glenn's flight, fraught with more dangers than were admitted beforehand, showed that the *Mercury* capsule in which he flew could withstand the enormous temperatures of re-entry from actual orbit. Glenn went on to be elected a U.S. senator from Ohio four times, beginning in 1974. At seventy-seven, Glenn became the oldest person to make a space flight as one of a crew of seven aboard the shuttle *Discovery*, October 29 through November 7, 1998.

282.

1962—*SILENT SPRING*

In 1962, Rachel Carson published a best-selling book called *Silent Spring* that gave detailed evidence of the harm to all forms of life being caused by chemical pesticides, particularly DDT. The most influential exposé of its kind since Upton Sinclair's *The Jungle* in 1906 had led to regulation of the meat-packing industry and the formation of the Food and Drug Administration, *Silent Spring* warned of the day when no bird would sing unless steps were taken to control the proliferation of harmful chemicals. This clarion call for conservation deeply alarmed Americans, and would lead to the eventual outlawing of DDT in the United States, but many of the book's ideas were strongly contested by numerous industries. To this day, the environmental movement, large and powerful as it has become, particularly in western states, must fight for every new control.

283.

1963—*THE FEMININE MYSTIQUE*

Betty Friedan was a housewife and a mother of three, but she also found time to write a book, published in 1963, that would become a major bestseller and a philosophical lodestone for the women's liberation movement. *The Feminine Mystique* was a frontal attack on the idea that women could find fulfillment only through childbearing and homemaking. It proposed that in order to find personal fulfillment, it was necessary for women to have something aside from their husbands and children to be concerned about, preferably a job that made use of whatever particular talents they had. The book gave numerous examples of women whose relationships with their families had actually improved once they found a sustaining interest outside the family. Her book stood in stark contrast to a bestseller of the previous year, *Sex and the Single Girl,* by Helen Gurley Brown, who would go on to become the very successful editor of *Cosmopolitan* magazine, which focused on how to get a man. Mrs. Friedan would subsequently become the founder of the National Organization for Women in 1966. But although she sought a new role for women, and was a role model for many, she was in many ways a moderate and would later deplore the extremes of radical feminism. She sought a new role for women, not a rejection of anything male.

284.

1963—THE MARCH ON WASHINGTON

On August 28, 1963, more than 200,000 African Americans and many white supporters of civil rights gathered in Washington, D.C., in peaceful assembly to demonstrate for their cause. The marchers completely covered the area around the Reflecting Pool, all the way from the Lincoln Memorial to the Washington Monument. There were many speakers that day, but the chief address was given by the Reverend Dr. Martin Luther King, Jr. His "I have a dream . . ." speech has been recognized as one of the greatest in American history, and its message of freedom and justice for the black citizens of the United States resounds to this day.

285.

1963 — PRESIDENT KENNEDY ASSASSINATED

At the beginning of the century, in 1901, President William McKinley was assassinated. Shocking though the event was, there was no radio to report the awful event quickly, and there was no television to show it actually occurring. When President John F. Kennedy was assassinated on November 22, 1963, in Dallas, Texas, the whole world knew about it instantly, and the Zapruder film would soon show the President physically recoil as he was hit. For the first time in history, the assassination of a major political leader had been brought right into everyone's living room, and the impact reverberates to this day. Kennedy was only forty-six when he was killed, and had been in office just over a thousand days. His youth and abbreviated tenure as president as well as the fact that he had two children under ten, Caroline and John, added to the horror of his death. The televised images of his wife, Jackie, in her blood-stained pink suit, and of three-year-old John-John saluting his father's coffin as the funeral procession, led by the new president, Lyndon Johnson, and the leaders of the world, passed down Pennsylvania Avenue have become indelible memories to all who witnessed them.

286.

1964—THE BEATLES COME TO AMERICA

The young group of rock singers from Liverpool, England, known as the Beatles were scheduled to make their first American appearances in February 1964. The president of Capitol Records, their U.S. label, told the press, "We don't think they'll do anything in this market." Never was a man happier to be wrong. From the moment of their arrival in New York on February 7, they were given the kind of hysterical adoration that had previously greeted Frank Sinatra during his New York concerts in 1942, and Elvis Presley following his debut on the *Ed Sullivan* show in 1954. Sullivan had the Beatles on, too; the audience screamed so much they could hardly be heard, but John Lennon, Paul McCartney, George Harrison, and Ringo Starr were on their way to a level of commercial and artistic success enjoyed by no other singing group of the century. Within a short time, they had become the number one British export, singlehandedly improving Great Britain's economic balance of payments. Unusual for a top popular group, they also wowed the critics, many of whom called their 1967 album *Sergeant Pepper's Lonely Hearts Club Band* the greatest pop disk ever produced.

287.

1964—RANGER 7 TRANSMITS PHOTOS OF MOON

On July 31, 1964, *Ranger 7*, a robot craft equipped with cameras, transmitted four thousand pictures of the surface of the moon back to earth, surveying a potential landing site for an eventual manned craft. The photographs thrilled scientists; they were a thousand times as clear as any ever obtained of the moon through earth-based telescopes. The still pictures were taken and transmitted during a seventeen-minute window of opportunity as the craft swept over the moon's surface before crashing into it, as planned.

288.

1964—KHRUSHCHEV OUSTED AS SOVIET LEADER

Americans, who had feared and despised Joseph Stalin and were often unsure what to make of other Soviet leaders, were fascinated by Nikita Khrushchev. He had become the top Soviet leader in 1957 and the American public was amused by his "kitchen debate" with Vice President Richard Nixon in Moscow in 1959. His espousal of "peaceful coexistence" with the United States and his 1959 visit to the United States encouraged hopes of peace, despite his famous shoe banging exhibition at the United Nations during that trip. The Cuban missile crisis of 1962, which put the United States and the Soviet Union on the brink of nuclear war was frightening, but the fact that Khrushchev backed down was reassuring in the aftermath. Backing down cost him heavily in Moscow, however, and combined with crop failures and a rift with China, led to his expulsion as leader on October 15, 1964.

289.

1964—WARREN COMMISSION REPORT

On September 24, 1964, after a ten-month review of the facts, private hearings, and new investigations, the Warren Commission's report on its official inquiry into the assassination of President John F. Kennedy was issued. It concluded that Lee Harvey

Oswald had been acting on his own in shooting the president from the School Book Depository in Dallas, Texas, on November 22, 1963. Headed by Earl Warren, the Chief Justice of the United States, the blue-ribbon panel clearly expected that its voluminous report would put the matter to rest. It did nothing of the kind. In the ensuing decades, hundreds of books have been written in an attempt to prove that there was in fact a conspiracy. Unfortunately, almost every book came up with a different answer to what that conspiracy consisted of and who was behind it. Oliver Stone's 1991 movie *JFK* further inflamed the debate. Whatever the truth, a majority of Americans have made clear in poll after poll that they do not accept the Warren Report conclusion that Oswald was a "lone gunman."

290.

1964—LYNDON JOHNSON WINS
LANDSLIDE VICTORY

Although the Vietnam War was already under way, Lyndon Johnson's handling of the presidency following Kennedy's assassination, and the appeal of his "Great Society" programs, brought him an even bigger landslide victory than either of Eisenhower's massive wins. He was helped by the fact that the Republicans nominated the outspoken conservative Senator Barry Goldwater of Arizona. Goldwater was easy to paint as an extremist with a nuclear trigger finger, and Johnson won by 486 electoral votes to 52. Ironically, in the decade before his death in 1998, Goldwater often infuriated right-wing Republicans by taking centrist or even "liberal" positions, such as supporting the right to abortion and the right for homosexuals to serve in the military. But in 1964, Goldwater had made the voters extremely nervous with what then seemed right-wing positions.

291.

1965—EARLY BIRD COMMUNICATIONS SATELLITE

In 1965, American television began to make use of the Early Bird communications satellite that had been launched by the United States government, employing it to bring feeds from its foreign correspondents. The idea for communications satellites had first been suggested twenty years earlier by a young Royal Air Force radar technician named Arthur C. Clarke. He had just begun publishing science-fiction short stories, but he also wrote technical scientific articles. The concept of communications satellites was put forward in one article called "Extra-Terrestrial Relays," which appeared in an obscure journal and was paid little attention to at the time. Those who did take note of it tended to see it more as fiction than science. However, in the article Clarke had set down what he believed to be the best possible orbit in which to place a communications satellite. The Early Bird satellites, and many later ones, were placed in precisely the orbit young Clarke had suggested, and that orbit carries his name. Clarke, of course, also went on to become one of the major science-fiction writers of the century, with classics such as *Childhood's End* and *2001: A Space Odyssey* to his credit.

292.

1965—THE GREAT BLACKOUT

On the evening of November 9, 1965, the greatest power failure in history blacked out almost all of New York City, parts of nine northeastern states, and two provinces of Canada, affecting at least twenty-five million people. In New York City alone, 800,000 people were trapped in the subways at rush hour. There were no riots during the blackout, and very little looting took place. Citizens manned busy corners to direct traffic, and emergency crews worked to free those trapped in subways and elevators. Surprising good spirits prevailed, and a good deal of humor ensued. On a high floor of the Empire State Building, firemen pounded on the doors of an elevator and asked if any pregnant women were inside. A male voice jauntily replied, "Not yet," and female giggles could be heard. Another blackout would plunge New York City and parts of Westchester County into darkness in July 1977, but the blackout of 1965 remains the most massive failure of modern technology.

293.

1965—*GEMINIS* IN SPACE RENDEZVOUS

On December 15, 1965, two American *Gemini* craft, with Captain Walter M. Schirra, Jr., and Major Thomas P. Stafford aboard *Gemini 6,* and Lieutenant Colonel Frank Borman and Commander James A. Lovell, Jr., on *Gemini 7,* made history with the first rendezvous in space between separate craft. Traveling as close as six to ten feet from each other, the space vessels circled the earth nearly two times 185 miles up. This close approach was a vital step toward the eventual rendezvous and docking of the *Apollo* moon craft and their moon landers.

294.

1966—DRAFT PROTESTS

In 1965, the U.S. Army draft had called up about five thousand men a month. Less than a year later, the call-up was almost ten times as high, and young men in college were no longer exempt from fighting in Vietnam. The protests that resulted were on a scale that had never been seen before. There had been a few draft riots at the beginning of the Civil War, but only isolated incidents during the century's two world wars. Now students were massing on college campuses and marching in city streets chanting, "Hell, no, we won't go!"

In 1966, 35,000 men and women of all ages marched on the Pentagon to protest the Vietnam War, and were met by an army of military police with rifles at the ready. The protestors mockingly stuffed flowers into the barrels of the guns; Norman Mailer caught the atmosphere of the day in his highly acclaimed book *The Armies of the Night*, published in 1968. By then more than 10,000 young American men had become not just draft protestors but draft dodgers, most of them fleeing to Canada, where organizations like the Toronto Student Unions for Peace helped them to adjust to their self-imposed exile.

295.

1966—MIRANDA RIGHTS

On June 13, 1966, the United States Supreme Court issued a ruling, written by Chief Justice Earl Warren, declaring that the police must always inform a suspect of his/her right to remain silent and to have legal counsel at the moment of arrest. The ruling reversed the conviction of a man named Ernesto Miranda in Arizona on the grounds that he had not been told of his rights before confessing to the crime. What came to be called Miranda rights have been a thorn in the side of law enforcement agencies ever since. This "coddling of criminals," as opponents called it, added new fuel to the calls for the impeachment of Chief Justice Warren that had begun with the 1954 *Brown* v. *Board of Education* decision outlawing school segregation. But Warren did not retire until 1969, when he was seventy-seven.

296.

1966 — THE "CULTURAL REVOLUTION" IN CHINA

The founder of the People's Republic of China, Mao Tse-tung, had been replaced as chairman of China in 1959 following the failure of the program for economic growth called "The Great Leap Foward." He was replaced as chairman by Liu Shao-ch'i, but retained his party leadership post. From that position, Mao launched the "Cultural Revolution." Revolutionary Red Guards, recruited among the young, attacked so-called bourgeois elements in the national leadership, leading to the death or exile of many intellectuals. The movement became so violent and created so much disorder, however, that it had to be reined in, and was halted in 1969. In the meantime, however, Liu Shao-ch'i had been removed from power in 1968, putting Mao once again in place as China's most powerful leader.

297.

1967—SIX-DAY WAR IN MIDDLE EAST

War between Israel and the Arab states of the United Arab Republic (Egypt), Syria, Jordan, and Lebanon broke out on June 5, 1967. The Israeli forces, directed by Defense Minister Moshe Dayan, routed the Arab countries on all sides. By the end of the Six-Day War, on June 10, Israel controlled the Sinai Peninsula, the Gaza Strip, and Old Jerusalem. These areas would subsequently become the basis for more than thirty years of intermittent peace negotiations, still ongoing in 1999, during which Israel would return various parcels of land in exchange for guarantees of peace. The "Land for Peace" equations would dominate Israeli foreign policy from then on.

298.

1967—THURGOOD MARSHALL BECOMES FIRST
BLACK ON SUPREME COURT

Thurgood Marshall, the courtly, scholarly attorney who had successfully argued the *Brown* v. *Board of Education* case that ended public school segregation in 1954, was chosen by President Johnson in 1967 to serve as a justice on the Supreme Court, before which he had often argued so eloquently for the civil rights of black Americans. He would serve with distinction until 1991, when he retired due to illness. He was replaced by another black justice, Clarence Thomas, who was as conservative as Marshall was liberal. That in itself was a sign of how much things had changed for black Americans since Marshall gained his 1954 school desegregation victory.

299.

1967—FIRST HEART TRANSPLANT

On December 3, 1967, South African surgeon Christiaan Barnard performed the first transplant of a human heart. The donor was a twenty-five-year-old woman named Denise Darvall, who had been fatally injured when hit by a car. She was clinically dead of head injuries, but physicians kept her heart pumping until the recipient, Louis Washkansky, a fifty-three-year-old grocer, could have his chest opened to receive the new heart. Barnard had made the decision to proceed about 9:00 P.M. on December 2; the operation was concluded at 5:34 A.M. on the third. The heart functioned perfectly, but Washkansky contracted pneumonia and died eighteen days later. However, the "impossible" had been achieved. Heart transplants are still far from routine operations, but they have become more common, and even simultaneous heart-lung transplants have a high success rate.

300.

1968—MARTIN LUTHER KING, JR., ASSASSINATED

In Memphis, Tennessee, on April 4, 1968, the Reverend Dr. Martin Luther King, Jr., was shot to death on a motel balcony. America's foremost civil rights leader, who had always preached nonviolence and racial harmony, and who had won the Nobel Peace Prize in 1964, was killed by a high-powered rifle fired from some distance away. James Earl Ray, a white man, was convicted of the killing, but later recanted. Even the King family wanted him to have a new trial so that the full truth could be brought out; Ray died in prison in 1998 without ever testifying in any court. In the aftermath of King's assassination, riots broke out in several major cities, and the National Guard was called upon to restore order in Washington, D.C., Chicago, and other cities.

301.

1968—ROBERT F. KENNEDY ASSASSINATED

After giving a speech in a Los Angeles hotel ballroom to a cheering crowd celebrating his victory in the California Democratic presidential primary, Senator Robert F. Kennedy was shot in the kitchen area of the hotel while making his way out on June 6, 1968. Twenty hours later, he was dead of his wounds. As was the case with his brother, President John F. Kennedy, a lone assassin was charged with the crime. Sirhan B. Sirhan, an Arab immigrant from Jordan, was convicted and sentenced to life in prison. Coming on top of the assassination of Martin Luther King, Jr., in Memphis, Kennedy's death led President Johnson to appoint a special commission on violence in the United States. This dark year in American history would be further marred by a riot that broke out between Chicago police and antiwar demonstrators outside the Democratic national convention that summer.

302.

1968—RICHARD M. NIXON ELECTED PRESIDENT

Not since William Henry Harrison in 1840 had a candidate been defeated for the presidency only to win it on his second try. From that point of view alone, Richard M. Nixon's 1968 victory over the Democratic candidate, Hubert H. Humphrey, the incumbent vice president, was remarkable. But it was very close. Humphrey was closing in fast in the last days of the campaign, and many historians believe that if he had separated himself from President Johnson's Vietnam policy sooner than he did, he might well have won. As it was, Nixon's popular-vote plurality was just over 500,000 votes, although his electoral majority was 301 to 191, with 46 electoral votes going to the independent candidate, George C. Wallace of Alabama, a strong opponent of school desegregation.

303.

1968—*APOLLO* ASTRONAUTS ORBIT MOON

The dark year of 1968 got a lift at the very end when on Christmas Eve, Colonel Frank Borman, Major William A. Anders, and Captain James A. Lovell, Jr., became the first human beings to orbit the moon. After ten orbits aboard *Apollo 8*, the craft fired its rockets to boost it back toward the earth for a splashdown in the Pacific Ocean fifty-seven hours later. As *Apollo 8* started its return voyage, a voice from the craft, 231,000 miles away, could be heard saying, "Please be informed there is a Santa Claus."

304.

1969—MEN WALK ON MOON

Houston, Tranquility Base here. The Eagle has landed."
These words, radioed back to earth by Neil A. Armstrong, the civilian commander of *Apollo 11*, were the first to be heard from the surface of another world, marking the greatest achievement of technology, will, and human courage in the history of humankind. The entire world had watched the landing craft's descent to the moon's surface as its external cameras recorded the approach. Six and one half hours later, Neil Armstrong, once again pictured by the external cameras, was seen to step down onto the moon's surface, and was heard saying, "That's one small step for [a] man, one giant leap for mankind." Shortly thereafter, he was joined on the surface by Colonel Edwin E. Aldrin, Jr., while Captain Michael Collins orbited above them in the command capsule *Columbia*. An American flag was planted on the moon, a demonstration that the United States had won the space race with the Soviet Union, but the entire world was caught up in the wonder of that day, Sunday, July 20, 1969. One of the most implausible dreams of the ancients had become a reality.

305.

1970—OZONE LAYER WARNINGS

The first warning that the emissions from man-made machines could affect the stratospheric ozone layer that protects the earth from the sun's ultraviolet rays came in 1970. The issue was raised by Harold Johnston of the University of California at Berkeley, in regard to the planned Supersonic Transport, meant to be the American answer to the French-British Concorde, then in development. Two other chemists at the University of California at Irvine, F. Sherwood Rowland and Mario Molina, then concluded that chlorofluorocarbons (CFCs), used in the manufacture of many insulating plastics as well as in refrigerators and aerosol spray cans, were already damaging the ozone layer. One of the biggest fights between science and industry of the century was just getting started.

The scientists got the upper hand at first. The Supersonic Transport was canceled, and within four years the U.S. Congress had banned the use of CFCs in spray cans. But in the United States alone, CFCs were being used in industries worth $28 billion a year, and those industries fought back, lobbying Congress hard to forestall further restrictions. The discovery of the ozone hole over Antarctica in 1985 once more gave the scientists the upper hand, and in 1987 the Montreal Protocol limiting the production of CFCs was signed by forty-seven countries. Science had created CFCs, and scientists led the fight to control them. It was the kind of scenario that had earlier been played out in respect to atomic bombs, and one that could not have played out in any previous century.

306.

1971—COMMUNIST CHINA ADMITTED TO THE UNITED NATIONS

In a late-night session on October 25, 1971, the General Assembly voted to admit Communist China to the United Nations and to expel the Chinese Nationalists of Taiwan. By a vote of seventy-six to thirty-five, with seventeen abstentions, the United Nations thus finally achieved what the United States had been trying to prevent for twenty-two years. George Bush, who had served as the United States envoy to China, and was now the chief U.S. delegate to the United Nations, called the vote a "moment of infamy." But twenty years later, as president, he would work hard to normalize relations with Communist China.

307.

1972—U.S./SOVIET ARMS AGREEMENT

For the first time since the dropping of the first atomic bomb on Hiroshima in 1945, a step was taken toward curtailing the likelihood of nuclear war on May 27, 1972. The development of atomic and hydrogen bombs had proceeded apace since 1945, and the nuclear arms race between the United States and the Soviet Union had produced a situation in which the two countries possessed enough bombs to destroy one another totally several times over. In late May 1972, in Moscow, President Nixon and Soviet party leader Leonid I. Brezhnev signed a treaty that for the first time put limits on the growth of the U.S. and Soviet strategic nuclear arsenals. Other such agreements would follow, and real progress toward nuclear disarmament would occur following the collapse of the Soviet Union in 1991. By then, however, many other nations had developed nuclear bombs or were on the verge of doing so.

308.

1972—U.S. SUPREME COURT BARS
DEATH PENALTY

In a 5–4 decision on June 29, 1972, the U.S. Supreme Court found the death penalty unconstitutional on the grounds that it violated the Eighth Amendment protection against "cruel and unusual punishment." All five of the justices in the majority wrote separate opinions, and seemed to agree on little except that the death penalty was unconstitutional because it was applied so erratically. The lack of support for any single line of reasoning, however, illuminated the problems that remained on the Court concerning this question. And indeed the death penalty would be reinstated by the Court, whose membership had changed, in 1987.

309.

1972—EQUAL RIGHTS AMENDMENT

Since the ratification of the Nineteenth Amendment, giving women the vote, in 1920, the main objective of many women's groups had been the passage of an equal rights amendment clearly stating that women had equality before the law in every way. The amendment was passed by the U.S. Congress in 1972, but failed to be ratified by a sufficient number of states. Part of the problem was the backlash by many conservatives, including such women as Phyllis Schlafly, against "women's libbers," part was due to so many women's rights having already become law, and part was because complete equality, as defined by this Twenty-seventh Amendment, also raised the question of the possibility of new duties and risks, such as women being drafted into the armed services. Despite the fact that Congress subsequently voted to extend the time allowed for ratification, the Twenty-seventh Amendment could not muster the support of the required two thirds of the states, and it expired in 1982 without ratification.

310.

1972—ISRAELI OLYMPIANS KILLED

The darkest hour of the modern Olympic Games occurred on September 6, 1972. The 1936 Games, with Adolf Hitler as host, had been highly controversial, and the Olympics had been suspended during both world wars, but the killing of nine Israeli athletes, and the wounding of two others, by four Arab terrorists in 1972 was a moment of utter horror. The fact that the Games were taking place in Germany, at Munich, for the first time since the Holocaust of World War II in which six million Jews were put to death, added a particular sense of outrage. The Games were initially suspended in the wake of the Israeli deaths, but then resumed in tribute to the fallen athletes and as a signal that terrorism could not prevail.

311.

1972—NIXON REELECTED IN LANDSLIDE

Although the early signs of the Watergate scandal that would eventually drive Richard Nixon from office were already apparent, he was reelected by a huge majority, taking 520 electoral votes to a mere 17 for the Democratic candidate, Senator George McGovern of South Dakota. The leader of the left-wing reformist faction of the Democratic party, and a strong opponent of the Vietnam War, McGovern was painted as an extremist, just as Republican Barry Goldwater had been, on the right instead of the left, in 1964. And as had happened with Goldwater, McGovern would eventually come to be seen not as an extremist but as an independent voice for common sense. Both men were in some respects ahead of their times.

312.

1973—STEPHEN SONDHEIM ASCENDANT

In 1971, the composer/lyricist Stephen Sondheim won the Tony Award for Best Score of a Musical for *Company;* in 1972, he won for *Follies;* and in 1973, he won for *A Little Night Music.* No composer in Broadway history, before or since, has won three such awards in a row. Sondheim was accused by some critics of being too cynical, of not showing enough feeling, but he had demonstrated with his lyrics to Leonard Bernstein's score for 1957's *West Side Story* that his lyrics could soar. And his first solo success, 1963's much-revived *A Funny Thing Happened on the Way to the Forum,* showed that he could be as funny as anyone on Broadway. But he was after something new, and in show after show over the second half of the century, he gave audiences something different every time. He has been called the "Mozart of the Twentieth Century," by people who remember that Mozart wrote his operas for popular theaters; indeed, a number of Sondheim musicals, including *A Little Night Music, Sweeney Todd* (1979), and the Pulitzer Prize–winning (with James Lapire) *Sunday in the Park With George* (1985), have been produced by opera houses. Sondheim himself has immense respect for such great predecessors as Jerome Kern, Irving Berlin, and Richard Rodgers and Oscar Hammerstein (in fact, Hammerstein was his mentor), but it seems likely that Sondheim's works will have the longest life of any of them.

313.

1973—VICE PRESIDENT AGNEW RESIGNS

For the first time in American history, a vice president of the United States was forced to resign. Spiro Agnew admitted evading taxes in 1967 when he was governor of Maryland, pleading no contest to the charge. In return for resigning, he was fined and given probation instead of standing trial. In a Washington torn apart by charges that President Nixon had orchestrated a cover-up in the Watergate case, this new bombshell left politicians reeling. Within two days, however, President Nixon nominated the Republican House minority leader, Gerald R. Ford of Michigan, as vice president, following confirmation by the U.S. Congress under the new succession rules of the Twenty-fifth Amendment, adopted in 1967. Ford was sworn in on December 6, 1973.

314.

1974 — PRESIDENT NIXON RESIGNS

It had begun with a "second-rate burglary" of the offices of the Democratic National Committee in 1972. The burglars were caught and convicted, but one of them, James McCord, tipped off the judge in the case, John Sirica, that an enormous cover-up involving highly placed officials was taking place. The subsequent investigation discovered that the trail led directly to the White House. A special bipartisan Senate committee headed by Senator Sam Ervin was told by former White House counsel John Dean that high officials, including the attorney general and former Nixon law partner John Mitchell, had been aware of the burglary before it happened. To the nation's astonishment, it also came out that President Nixon had audio tapes of all Oval Office conversations. Nixon's refusal to turn over the tapes, and his firing of Special Prosecutor Archibald Cox, led to a constitutional confrontation that ended when the U.S. Supreme Court ordered Nixon to surrender the tapes. A subsequent House Judiciary Committee hearing adopted three impeachment articles against President Nixon, but before they could be voted on by the full House (passage would have brought an impeachment trial in the Senate), Nixon resigned on August 4, 1974, the first president to relinquish the presidency in this manner.

315.

1 9 7 5 — W A T E R G A T E   C O N S P I R A T O R S   G U I L T Y

In 1975, the highest placed of the Nixon administration members implicated in the Watergate scandal were found guilty. H. R. Haldeman and John D. Ehrlichman, President Nixon's two closest White House aides, and former attorney general and Nixon law partner John N. Mitchell were all sentenced to prison. Judge John J. Sirica sentenced the men to not less than thirty months and not more than eight years, but later reduced the sentences to one to four years, feeling that the point had been made about the consequences of breaking the law even at the highest levels of government. The three men were paroled in 1978. The long nightmare of the Watergate scandal was finally at an end, but the repercussions of the special-prosecutor law created to deal with it would continue to be felt for the rest of the century, coming to a head during the Clinton administration.

316.

1 9 7 5 — M I C R O S O F T   F O U N D E D

The credit line in the source code for the first product produced by Microsoft, the fledgling software company founded in 1975, read: "Micro-Soft BASIC: Bill Gates wrote a lot of stuff; Paul Allen wrote some other stuff." The name would soon be changed slightly (the hyphen was taken out), but it wouldn't be until 1981 that Gates and Allen would actually get around to incorporating their company, two years after they moved their headquarters from Albuquerque, New Mexico, to a suburb of Seattle, where both had grown up. Bill Gates was only nineteen, and Paul Allen only twenty-one when they recognized the importance that computer software would soon have and decided to start creating it. By 1997, Bill Gates was the world's richest man, and Paul Allen, even though he had withdrawn from active running of the company in 1982, when he began successful treatment for Hodgkin's disease, was also a billionaire many times over from his Microsoft holdings and other, later investments. Microsoft Windows would come to be so ubiquitous as a fundamental computer software platform that the U.S. Justice Department has sought an antitrust judgment against the company—litigation that is likely to last for many years. However it turns out, Bill Gates is already assured recognition as the century's most successful entrepreneur.

317.

1976—*VIKING 1* LANDS ON MARS

On July 20, 1976, the first successful landing on the planet Mars by a craft launched from earth was made by *Viking 1*. The NASA craft, a squat three-legged robot, came to rest in an upright position on the Chryse Plain of Mars at 7:53 A.M., Eastern Standard Time. Over the previous eleven months, the craft had traveled nearly half a billion miles in an approach designed to intersect with Mars that would make a soft landing possible. Eight years in the making, the *Viking* immediately started transmitting spectacular photographs of the rocky Martian surface back to Earth. Two previous Soviet efforts had failed to provide usable data, but the *Viking* gave humankind its first close-up look at the surface of the red planet, the nearest to Earth in the solar system and an object of human conjecture since time immemorial.

318.

1976—ORDINATION OF WOMEN AS EPISCOPAL PRIESTS

On September 16, 1976, the Episcopal Church in the United States, at a meeting of its bishops, voted to approve the ordination of women as full-fledged Episcopal priests. The Episcopal Church thus took the lead on an issue that has roiled many denominations in the last quarter of the century. Even among Episcopalians, the move was not universally viewed as a good one, and a splinter group broke away from the denomination the following year. That has proved to be the case in several other denominations. As late as 1998, there was a similar rift among Presbyterians. Many religious groups have steadfastly resisted the ordination of women, with Pope John Paul II going so far in 1998 as to forbid further discussion of the issue; the Southern Baptists have also stood strongly against having women as ministers. But the step taken by the Episcopalians in 1976 is generally regarded as having strengthened that denomination, and it seems inevitable that the push to make such a change will continue in many religions well into the next century.

319.

1976—JIMMY CARTER ELECTED PRESIDENT

James Earl Carter, Jr., who insisted on being called Jimmy, was an obscure ex-governor of Georgia in 1975. Less than two years later he was president of the United States. His campaign to win the Democratic nomination was one of the most spectacular "coming from nowhere" efforts in American history. His victory over President Gerald Ford was fairly close, however; he took 297 electoral votes to Ford's 241. Ford had been hampered by the fact that he was the first unelected president, chosen by Congress under the new Twenty-fifth Amendment to replace Spiro Agnew, who had resigned in a kickback scandal. Ford had then become president when Richard Nixon resigned, and had hurt himself by giving Nixon a presidential pardon. He was also severely challenged by California Governor Ronald Reagan for the nomination. All these factors helped to give the previously little known Jimmy Carter an edge.

320.

1977—VIETNAM DRAFT EVADERS PARDONED

Early in his first year as president, Jimmy Carter pardoned those who had evaded the Vietnam War draft, either by going underground in the United States, or, more commonly, fleeing to other countries, particularly Canada. While this pardon drew howls of protest from conservatives of both parties, Carter saw it as a necessary first step in healing the still raw social and political wounds affecting the people of the United States. Polls of the public supported him—the majority of Americans wanted to start putting the horrors of Vietnam behind them.

321.

1977—PANAMA CANAL TREATY

On September 7, 1973, President Jimmy Carter signed the Panama Canal Treaty, which would return control of the Canal to the country of Panama on December 31, 1999. The Canal had been one of the great engineering feats of the century, and its strategic importance to the United States had been regarded as enormous, in terms of both the movement of American naval vessels and commercial ships from one coast of the United States to the other. Its strategic importance had declined somewhat with the development of container cargo ships too large to make use of it, and it had never been capable of providing passage to aircraft carriers. However, it remained a potent symbol of U.S. power, and conservative forces fought hard against giving it up. When the treaty seemed doomed to defeat, help came from a highly unlikely source. The movie star John Wayne, one of the most conservative people in Hollywood and an icon to conservative voters and politicians, wrote a letter urging passage of the treaty, and telling the leader of the opposition, Senator Barry Goldwater, the right-wing Republican presidential candidate in 1964, that he was wrong. Wayne had been married to three women of Latin descent, and had had homes in Central and South America. He understood that if the treaty failed it would cause lasting damage to relations between the United States and Latin America. His letter swayed just enough votes to bring about the narrow passage of the treaty by the Senate.

322.

1977—THE *GOSSAMER CONDOR*

One of humankind's most ancient dreams had been to fly, and before the invention of the combustion engine, most such attempts (aside from balloon flights) involved trying to develop a winged machine that could be kept aloft by the power of human muscle. All failed. Men did fly, beginning with the Wright brothers, and developed jet planes and rockets that carried astronauts to the moon. Still, no one had succeeded in flying a machine powered by sheer muscle. The age-old dream was finally realized in 1977, when an aeronautical engineer and three-time National Soaring Champion in gliders, Paul MacCready, achieved the impossible. Building a glider of new superlight materials, and equipping it with pedal mechanics, he launched himself from a hillside and pedaled in a figure-eight pattern for a full mile above California's San Joaquin Valley. The machine he flew was called the *Gossamer Condor*, in honor of California's endangered bird species. Two years later, he flew a second machine across the entire English Channel under his own muscle power. This aircraft was named the *Gossamer Albatross,* in honor of Coleridge's *Rime of the Ancient Mariner.* MacCready's efforts, while hardly of technological significance in terms of future developments, were as fine a tribute to the spirit of invention as the Wright brothers' flight at the beginning of the century.

323.

1978—JOHN PAUL II

When the Italian cardinal Albino Luciani was elected pope following the death of Pope Paul VI in August 1978, he took the name John Paul to indicate that he would steer a path between the liberalism of John XXIII and Paul VI. He reigned as pope only thirty-four days, his death arousing suspicions in some quarters about the reasons for his demise—more than one book was published suggesting that he had been murdered because it had been discovered he was too liberal. In the midst of the uproar surrounding his death, the College of Cardinals met for the second time in two months to elect a new pope. To the astonishment of the world, a non-Italian was named, the first since 1522. Cardinal Karol Wojtyla, the archbishop of Krakow in Poland, soon demonstrated the reasons for his elevation. With a command of several languages, an imposing bearing, and conservative views, he became one of the most personally popular popes of the century. The fact that he was a native of a Communist-dominated country put him at the center of foreign affairs, and he traveled to more foreign countries than any pope in history. John Paul's robust physique, strengthened by the athleticism of his youth, made it possible for him to recover from serious wounds suffered in an assassination attempt in 1981 by a Turkish terrorist. Having appointed large numbers of conservative cardinals, he has made certain that his influence will be felt well into the twenty-first century.

324.

1978—THE CAMP DAVID ACCORDS

Trying to bring about a peace agreement between Israel and Egypt, President Jimmy Carter took Prime Minister Menachem Begin of Israel and President Anwar Sadat of Egypt to the presidential retreat Camp David in Maryland and kept them at the negotiating table from the fifth through the seventeenth of September, 1978. When they emerged, Begin and Sadat had signed an accord ending thirty years of hostility between the two countries. Begin and Sadat were awarded the Nobel Peace Prize, jointly, in 1978. Many people thought that President Carter should have shared in the award, but his work in bringing about the Camp David Accords established a diplomatic authority that enabled him to serve as a broker in many international disputes long after his presidency was over.

325.

1979—THREE MILE ISLAND NUCLEAR ACCIDENT

On March 28, 1979, there was a serious nuclear accident at the power plant located at Three Mile Island in eastern Pennsylvania. The drama of this accident was increased by the fact that a movie called *The China Syndrome*, starring Jane Fonda and Jack Lemmon, about the near-meltdown of a nuclear plant, had opened nationally just twelve days earlier. The core did not melt at Three Mile Island, but the accident made the plant unusable and caused panic in the immediate area and deep alarm in the communities surrounding nuclear plants all across the country. No new construction on a nuclear power plant has begun in the United States since 1979, and several plants then under construction were never completed. There are still many scientists who believe in nuclear power, and who think it is perfectly safe when proper safeguards exist, but public opinion takes a very different view.

326.

1979—MARGARET THATCHER BECOMES PRIME MINISTER OF GREAT BRITAIN

On May 4, 1979, Conservative party leader Margaret Thatcher became the first woman to serve as prime minister of Great Britain. In 1975, following the defeat of the Conservatives in the general election the previous year, she became party leader by defeating former Prime Minister Edward Heath on the first ballot at the party leadership elections. As opposition leader from 1975 to 1979, she had earned the nickname the "Iron Lady," and her tenure as prime minister, the longest in the twentieth century, was marked by many abrasive debates, not only with the Labour opposition but with members of her own party. She was finally dislodged as the leader of the Conservative party in 1991, and succeeded by one of her main protégés, John Major, as both party leader and prime minister. Her long period in office was one of economic austerity, strong foreign policy, and the undoing of much the welfare state created by the Labour party. One after another, industries, from coal production to water supply, that had been nationalized by the Labour party were returned to the private sector. "Thatcherism" created an entirely different Great Britain than had existed when she took power.

327.

1979—THE HOSTAGES IN IRAN

In November 1979, in reaction to the fact that the deposed shah of Iran had been permitted to enter the United States for cancer treatment, Iranian students seized the United States Embassy in Tehran, taking sixty-three U.S. citizens and forty other individuals hostage. The takeover of the embassy took place on November 4. Two days later, Ayatollah Khomeini's Islamic Revolutionary Council took power in Iran, ousting a provisional government. Khomeini backed the students to the hilt, and one of the great diplomatic crises of the century was under way. President Carter tried every diplomatic move possible to free the hostages before breaking off relations with Iran in April 1980 and sending in a failed commando mission to attempt a rescue by force. He was still negotiating the release of the hostages as he left the White House on Inauguration Day 1981 to see his successor in the White House, Ronald Reagan, take the oath of office. The hostages were released later that day. Carter's reelection chances had been severely damaged by the hostage crisis, and the Ayatollah's final insult was to release the hostages to his successor. President Reagan, however, properly sent Carter to Germany to greet them upon their release.

328.

1980—THE WALKMAN

The Japanese electronics giant Sony introduced a new product in 1980 that would have a sweeping success around the globe, particularly with the young. Called the Walkman, it was a light, compact tape player that could be carried in a pocket and listened to with headphones while walking along the street. Some people even listened to it while driving, but governments around the world moved to make that illegal because the headphones reduced the possibility of responding to traffic noise almost to nothing, greatly increasing the chance of accidents. Nevertheless, few electronic gadgets ever had such a rapid and huge success.

329.

1980—MICROBES CAN BE PATENTED

On June 16, 1980, in *Diamond* v. *Chakabarty*, the United States Supreme Court ruled that a microbe created by genetic engineering could be patented. This ruling opened the way to greatly increased research in the field of genetic engineering, since the ability to patent the results of such work could ensure eventual profits from it. Great strides have been made in the field since, and many experts expect biogenetic engineering to be one of the most important growth industries of the twenty-first century.

330.

1980 — MOSCOW OLYMPICS BOYCOTTED

Because of the Soviet invasion of Afghanistan in December 1979, a boycott of the Summer Olympic Games scheduled for Moscow in the summer of 1980 was organized. Led by the United States, sixty-five countries stayed away from the Moscow Olympics, including such major competitors as West Germany, Japan, and Kenya. France and Great Britain did send their contingents, but even so the events turned into what amounted to a Communist Olympic Games. President Jimmy Carter's lead in developing the boycott left the American public with divided opinions on the subject, and it was one of several factors that contributed to his failure to win reelection that fall.

331.

1980 — RONALD REAGAN ELECTED PRESIDENT

Ronald Reagan gained the Republican nomination on his second try, and defeated President Jimmy Carter with a massive 489 electoral votes to 49. However, Reagan got just under 51 percent of the popular vote, while Carter took 41 percent and nearly 7 percent went to independent candidate John B. Anderson, an Illinois congressman whose votes came almost entirely from Carter's column. Carter was badly hurt by the ongoing hostage crisis in Iran, and by a sense that he hadn't lived up to his presidential promise.

332.

1981—FIRST SHUTTLE FLIGHT

On April 12, 1981, the United States' first space shuttle, named *Columbia*, was launched from the Kennedy Space Center with two astronauts aboard, Captain Robert L. Crippen of the U.S. Navy and civilian John W. Young. After two days in orbit, the reusable winged spaceship blasted out of orbit and returned to earth, making a safe, solid landing on a dry lakebed at Edwards Air Force Base in California. It was the first time in nearly six years that American astronauts had gone into space, following the end of the *Apollo* voyages to the moon. The flight of *Columbia* heralded a new era of routine space flights. The explosion of the *Challenger* shuttle on January 28, 1986, would interrupt the program for more than two years while the disaster was investigated and new safety devices and procedures were put in place. Although the *Challenger* explosion was major news at the time, it ultimately proved to be, like the fire that consumed *Apollo 3* on its launching pad in 1967, an interruption rather than a death blow to the program. In the years since, dozens of shuttle flights have conducted hundreds of scientific experiments and medical tests, as well as carrying satellites and the Hubble Space Telescope into orbit, and docking in space with the Russian *Mir* space station. The shuttle program has proved so successful in fact that it has to some degree had the unintended effect of creating public boredom with space travel.

333.

1981 — ABORTION APPROVED BY ITALIAN VOTERS

In the second half of the twentieth century, the right to abortion was approved in many countries around the world, some before and some after the landmark *Roe* v. *Wade* decision by the United States Supreme Court in 1973. But because of the strong opposition to abortion by the Roman Catholic Church, it was believed that legalization of abortion in Italy would be a long time in coming. However, in a 1981 referendum, Italian voters easily approved abortion. This development was an enormous embarrassment to the Vatican, which had found itself unable to defeat the prochoice forces even in its own backyard.

334.

1981 — AIDS OFFICIALLY RECOGNIZED

The U.S. Centers for Disease Control officially recognized the disease called AIDS in 1981. Acquired immune deficiency syndrome was caused, it was discovered, by a virus called HIV, the exact origins of which remain obscure, although it is believed to have mutated from a less virulent virus affecting African monkeys. The first hint that a new disease was at work came in 1977, when two men in New York City were diagnosed with a rare cancer called Kaposi's sarcoma. AIDS spread rapidly in the United States among homosexual men who practiced unsafe sex with multiple partners and among intravenous drug users. This pattern showed up in many other parts of the world; but in Africa and Asia in particular, the disease spread rapidly among heterosexuals. In America and European countries, women contracted AIDS from infected males, and it was passed on by pregnant women to their children in the womb.

In recent years, combinations of experimental drugs have been found to control the disease in many individuals, allowing them to live normal lives with the HIV virus present in their bodies, but without developing full-blown symptomatic AIDS. However, these drugs are expensive and their usefulness over time is not yet known. While the number of new cases of AIDS has diminished in the United States and some other highly developed nations, the epidemic is out of control in many underdeveloped parts of the world. No cure has yet been found, but research continues in pursuit of one as well as for a vaccine that would prevent infection.

335.

1981—FIRST WOMAN ON SUPREME COURT

President Ronald Reagan named Sandra Day O'Connor of Arizona to the United States Supreme Court; she was the first woman to become an associate justice. Approved by the Senate 99–0, she was expected to be a staunch conservative, and on many issues she proved to be so. But she was the crucial vote in turning back later attempts to override the *Roe* v. *Wade* decision of 1973 that had made abortion legal in the United States. Although she was willing to see access to abortion somewhat restricted, and approved laws requiring parental consent for minors that had been passed by some states, she refused to join her mentor, Chief Justice William Rehnquist, also of Arizona, in his desire to overturn the *Roe* decision altogether. By the 1990s, Justice O'Connor was widely regarded as a crucial swing vote on numerous issues before the Court. Like many justices before her, she had proved to have more complex and more flexible views than her supporters originally expected.

336.

1982 — "PAC-MAN OF THE YEAR"

The *Time* magazine "Man of the Year" for 1982 startled many people. It wasn't even a human being, but a computer with the game called "Pac-Man" on the screen. The game had become an enormous hit in the United States and many other countries, played on machines located in arcades, bars, and motel lobbies. This choice by the editors of *Time* proved to be extremely prescient. As personal computers came on the market in the 1980s, computer games became a multibillion-dollar business. Pac-Man, a relatively simple "chase" game, would be superseded by ever-more complex ones with increasingly sophisticated computer graphics that created entire fantasy landscapes in which players were faced with innumerable choices about how to proceed. As sophisticated as games of the late 1990s like Myst had become, the computer industry promised far more visually complex and challenging games in the future, with still experimental technology suggesting the creation of "virtual reality" games that would make the player feel as though he or she were *inside* the game world. Some visionaries in the computer industry believe that virtual-reality games will become to the twenty-first century what movies have been to the twentieth: a ubiquitous form of entertainment that at its best will also be an art form.

337.

1983 — *PIONEER 10* LEAVES SOLAR SYSTEM

Pioneer 10, launched in 1972, sent back the first close-up views of the planet Jupiter in December 1973. It continued to send back a tracking signal as it passed the outer planets one by one and finally departed the solar system altogether in 1983. It was a primitive machine by the standards of today, but it became the first human-made object to travel outward into the wider universe. It bore a plaque showing the location of the earth, the shape of the human body, and greetings from humankind.

338.

1983 — U.S. LOSES AMERICA'S CUP

For the first time since yachting's greatest race began in 1870, the United States failed to win the America's Cup in 1983. There had been a total of twenty-four challenges at slightly irregular intervals over those years, and an American yacht had always retained the cup. But as yachting technology improved, and more countries entered the competition, the race became tougher. In 1983, the cup was won by the yacht *Australia II* of that country. Although the United States would win the cup back with *Stars and Stripes* in 1987, notice had been served that another nation could win. The 1983 loss was actually good for the race, as extensive television coverage of it and subsequent challenges, and the increased sense of real international competition, greatly enhanced public interest in what had always been a sport for the very rich.

339.

1984—TORVILL AND DEAN FIND PERFECTION

Jayne Torvill and Christopher Dean, the British ice dancing team, gave a series of competition performances in 1984 that brought them worldwide acclaim and the highest marks ever awarded in the nearly hundred-year history of the sport of figure skating. Ice dancing is divided into three separate competition units: compulsory dances to judge technical ability, a set pattern dance (a tango one year, a waltz another) with original choreography, and a final free dance that gives the competitors the fullest opportunity to display their creativity. In 1984, at the European Championships, the World Championships, and the Olympics, Torvill and Dean received a total of fifty-nine perfect marks of 6.0 from the judges. They had received their first perfect mark at the British Championships in 1978, and in the course of their amateur career through 1984, they amassed 136 such 6.0s, an accomplishment no other skater, in any of the four competitive divisions, has come close to matching.

340.

1984—HOME VIDEO TAPING LEGAL

In the decision *Sony v. Universal Studios*, the U.S. Supreme Court ruled on January 17, 1984, that home video taping, using a VCR to record programs aired on television, was legal. Such tapes could not be resold or shown for profit, but they could be recorded at will for personal viewing pleasure at a later date. This ruling opened the way for a vast increase in the sale of VCRs and blank tapes, and has shaped the television industry in innumerable ways.

341.

1984 — BREAKUP OF AT&T

At the conclusion of the most important antitrust case against a monopolistic company since the dismantling of Standard Oil in 1911, the American Telephone & Telegraph Company, popularly known as Ma Bell, was forced to break itself into separate units. These included regional telephone companies (Baby Bells), a research company, and a long-distance company still called AT&T. This action fostered the creation of such competing long-distance companies as MCI and SPRINT. Within a dozen years, however, new technologies involving cable television and the rapid development of the Internet created a new alignment that led to approval for the Baby Bells to start growing bigger through acquisitions once again.

342.

1984 — REAGAN REELECTED BY HUGE MARGIN

After a serious recession, the economy began booming again by the end of 1983, and Reagan's great personal popularity allowed him to win reelection by the greatest electoral landslide in American history, 525 votes to 13 for Walter F. Mondale of Minnesota. As Jimmy Carter's vice president, Mondale had been given unprecedented access and numerous important jobs to carry out, and in many ways he was probably better prepared to be president than anyone in American history. He also chose the first female runningmate, Congresswoman Geraldine Ferraro of New York, whose presence on the ticket, poise, and winning personality initially caused great excitement. But she was plagued by controversy over her family finances, and Mondale ran a lackluster campaign. After running into some trouble in the first presidential debate, in which he seemed wan and out of touch, Reagan rebounded in the second debate and coasted to victory.

343.

1985—FAMINE IN ETHIOPIA

The twentieth century had been marked by many great famines, brought on by drought, war, population explosions, and combinations of all three in many of the less developed areas of the world. But television images of the 1985 famine in Ethiopia, with its heartwrenching shots of starving children, brought a worldwide outpouring of emotion and financial assistance. It soon became apparent that such famines were very difficult to deal with, no matter what the resources. Several major famines have occurred since then, particularly in Africa, but the public has become increasingly frustrated with the failure to get food to those who need it most. The world has discovered that it is as difficult to deal with famine at the end of the century as it was at the beginning.

344.

1986—SOVIETS LAUNCH *MIR* SPACE STATION

While the American space program had achieved man's great dream of being able to walk on the surface of the moon, the Soviet program had a major first of its own with the launching of the *Mir* space station on February 19, 1986. This orbiting laboratory has been used for a great many experiments, and has tested the ability of human beings to stay in space for long periods of time, with some Russian astronauts remaining aboard the *Mir* for more than a year. American astronauts have joined the Russians at the *Mir* in the 1990s. Although the station had many well-publicized problems, especially in recent years, it has paved the way for a future international space station. The eventual manned exploration of the solar system, and perhaps beyond it, will depend on the combined technologies in landing humans on other planetary surfaces and operating space stations in orbit around them.

345.

1986—ANTIAPARTHEID ACT PASSED
BY U.S. CONGRESS

With the achievement of greater racial equality under the law in the United States, mounting pressure persuaded the United States Congress to try to force an end to the rigid separation of the races in South Africa that went under the name of apartheid. Congress levied economic sanctions against South Africa that caused major U.S businesses such as General Motors to withdraw from that country. Other nations joined in the effort, and over the next four years it gradually had the desired effect—a rare case of economic sanctions actually working. By 1990, President F. W. de Klerk lifted the thirty-year ban on the black African National Congress, and released its leader, Nelson Mandela, from prison after twenty-seven years. Mandela and de Klerk then set about working on the political compromises that would end apartheid altogether and create a new country in which all racial groups could play an equal part. For their efforts, Mandela and de Klerk would share the 1993 Nobel Peace Prize.

346.

1988—THE GRAND SLAM PLUS

The first woman to win the Grand Slam of Tennis—the French Open, the Australian Open, the U.S. Open, and Wimbledon—in the same year was Maureen "Little Mo" Connolly of the United States, in 1953, with straight-set victories at all four events. England's Margaret Court won the Grand Slam in 1970, and Martina Navratilova won all four consecutively but not in the same year, adding the French Open at the beginning of 1984 to wins in the other three the previous year. In 1988, Germany's Steffi Graf went them all one better. Not only did she win the Grand Slam, but also took the gold medal in tennis at the Olympic Games in Seoul, South Korea.

347.

1988—GEORGE BUSH ELECTED PRESIDENT

While the vice presidency might seem the ideal position from which to run for president, when George Herbert Walker Bush captured the Republican nomination in 1988, no sitting vice president had gone on to win the presidency on his first try since Martin Van Buren in 1836. Much of the public regarded Bush as a fairly lackluster second fiddle to Ronald Reagan, and he was not a particularly good speaker. He compounded his problems by choosing as his running mate a young senator from Indiana, Dan Quayle, who seemed to have a special gift for putting his foot in his mouth. All of these problems could easily have defeated Bush, but the Democratic candidate, the attractive governor of Massachusetts, Michael Dukakis, ran what journalists and political professionals considered a disastrously low-key and badly planned campaign. Initially ahead in the polls by a comfortable margin, and despite a spirited last-minute effort, Dukakis was defeated by 426 electoral votes to 111. Still, he had done better than any Democrat since 1976, and managed to regain the support of many crucial "Reagan Democrats," who would prove vital in the 1992 election.

348.

1989—THE BERLIN WALL FALLS

As East Germany threw off the yoke of communism, its government announced the opening of the border with West Germany on November 9, 1989. The next day, authorities began to dismantle the Berlin Wall, which had divided East and West Berlin since 1961. Citizens of both East and West Berlin soon joined in tearing down the totalitarian barrier, and carrying home chunks of it as souvenirs. Small pieces of the Wall were also subsequently offered to collectors in the United States by mail order, complete with a certificate of authenticity. Less than a year later, at midnight October 2, East and West Germany were officially reunited, a cause for great joy and a subsequent economic headache for the new Germany, which was faced with the difficulties of bringing the standard of living of former East Germans up to that of West Germans.

349.

1990 — THE HUBBLE TELESCOPE

Named for Edwin Hubble, the astronomer who was the first to make clear, in 1925, that the universe consists of innumerable galaxies, the orbiting Hubble Space Telescope was launched in 1990, carried aloft by the shuttle *Discovery*. Once in place, it was found to have a fault in its main mirror. A space walk in 1994, however, corrected the flaw, and since then the Hubble has performed beyond expectations, providing scientists with views farther into space, and thus back in time toward the beginning of the universe, than ever before. The resulting astronomical bonanza has revealed a universe even more complex and bizarre than had been expected, causing the revision of many theories and the beginning of many new ones. For each mystery the Hubble has solved, it has uncovered a new one, providing a fitting conclusion to the century in which more advances were made in astronomy and astrophysics than in all the rest of human history combined.

350.

1990 — SURGERY ON THE UNBORN

At Grey's Hospital in London, England, the first surgery on an unborn child within its mother's womb was performed on January 30, 1990. Such operations have been performed numerous times since, although they remain too difficult to be common. Used to repair faulty heart valves and lung development, they also hold promise as a way to correct other birth defects. Inconceivable at the start of the twentieth century, surgery on the unborn stands as a measure of the extraordinary developments in medical technique over the past one hundred years.

351.

1990—LECH WALESA
ELECTED PRESIDENT
OF POLAND

Although he always claimed to be a simple workingman, Lech Walesa proved that there was little a workingman couldn't do. In August 1980, he organized Solidarity, an independent and self-governing trade union in the shipbuilding port of Gdansk, Poland. A general strike forced the Polish administrators to sign an agreement allowing the workers to organize freely. But the Communist government, taking its orders from Moscow, outlawed the union in 1981, and interned Walesa for a year. In 1983, he won the Nobel Peace Prize, and as Communist control of Poland disintegrated during the 1980s, he was at the forefront of the push for free elections. In December 1990, he won a landslide election to become the first president of a free Poland.

352.

1991—PAN AMERICAN AIRLINES CLOSED DOWN

Founded in 1927, the year of Charles Lindbergh's legendary transatlantic flight in the *Spirit of St. Louis,* Pan American Airlines went out of business in 1991. Many major airlines had merged or gone bankrupt in the previous few years, but Pan American was the most prestigious of all those that went under. Despite the fact that more people were flying more often than ever, the profit margins for airlines had been shrinking for years, and only the best-managed were able to survive. Pan American Airlines left behind a monument to its one-time primacy in the form of the Pan Am Building straddling Park Avenue above New York City's Grand Central Station. One of the great pioneers of commercial flight, Pan Am had been founded to take advantage of one of the most profound changes of the century, the ability to fly, but in the end it became a victim of the very pace of that change.

353.

1991—"OPERATION DESERT STORM"

In August 1990, Kuwait was annexed by Iraq and Iraqi forces massed on the borders of Saudi Arabia. To protect Saudi Arabia, and the flow of oil from the Middle East, President George Bush sent U.S. forces to that country. However, as Iraq's dictator, Saddam Hussein, continued to threaten other countries and refused to give up Kuwait, a U.S.-led coalition called "Operation Desert Storm" launched a major offensive to free Kuwait and destroy Saddam if possible. By February 27, 1991, Kuwait had been liberated, and President Bush announced an end to hostilities even though Saddam was still in place as the ruler of Iraq. The rapid success of U.S. forces in the Gulf War sent President Bush's poll ratings sky-high, but as it became clear that Saddam Hussein was still a major menace, leading to charges that the United States had ended the hostilities too soon, Bush's popularity fell and he was defeated in the 1992 election. Saddam Hussein continued to give the world, and the Clinton administration, major headaches in the succeeding years.

354.

1991—THE END OF THE SOVIET UNION

In 1985, Mikhail Gorbachev was named the first secretary of the Communist party in the Soviet Union, and he called for greater *glasnost*, "openness." Elected president on October 1, 1986, he pursued both *glasnost* and a policy of *perestroika*, "reconstruction." The changes he brought about were so profound that by December 1989, Gobachev and President Bush jointly announced an end to the Cold War. Over the next two years, the Soviet Union essentially dismantled itself. When Gorbachev won the Nobel Peace Prize in 1990, he was in the process of putting himself out of a job. The central government of the Soviet Union was suspended by parliament on September 2, 1991, and a new constitution was written. In early December, the leaders of the now independent countries of Russia, Belarus, and Ukraine signed an agreement to join a new Commonwealth of States, and eight of the other new republics joined on December 21. On December 25, 1991, Gorbachev resigned as president of the USSR, and the Soviet Union officially ceased to exist. Russia, led by President Boris Yeltsin, remained by far the most powerful of the countries that had made up the Soviet Union, although several other countries, including Ukraine and Belarus, had control over the nuclear missiles that had been situated on their territories.

355.

1992 — WILLIAM JEFFERSON CLINTON
ELECTED PRESIDENT

The popularity of President George Bush following the Gulf War of 1991 was so high that many prominent Democratic politicians decided not to challenge him. By the time Bush began to decline in the polls, it was too late to start a presidential campaign. The vacuum was filled by Bill Clinton, the young four-term governor of Arkansas. Despite charges and rumors of adultery, mitigated by the strong backing of his wife, Hillary Rodham Clinton, he captured the Democratic nomination with surprising ease. A great campaigner, he ran what many journalists regarded as the best Democratic campaign since the days of Franklin Delano Roosevelt. A third-party candidate, the quirky Texas billionaire Ross Perot, took 19 percent of the popular vote in the November election, but gained no electoral votes. Bill Clinton won 370 electoral votes to George Bush's 168, and took just over 43 percent of the popular vote, almost the same as that taken by Richard Nixon over Hubert Humphrey and George Wallace in 1968.

356.

1993—THE INTERNET

First there had been ARPANET, way back in 1969, a computer network designed under the auspices of the U.S. Defense Department to ensure that a nuclear attack would not wipe out all communications. A new language for these linked computers known as HTML (*Hyper-Text Markup Language*) was invented by Tim Berners-Lee at the European Laboratory for Particle Physics in Geneva, Switzerland. Using UNIX code, scientists at laboratories around the world could now trade information rapidly through the computer network, which had come to be known as the World Wide Web. But UNIX code was far too complex for the average person to use. Then a group of graduate students at the University of Illinois computer laboratories created a browser called Mosaic. Marc Andreessen, twenty-one years old, a friend named Eric Bina, and a few others who contributed ideas devised Mosaic in a two-month period and distributed it free over the World Wide Web, as HTML had been earlier. Anyone with a fundamental grasp of computer technology could use Mosaic. That was in the spring of 1993. At Microsoft, Bill Gates was slow to see the implications of the Internet, and then had to play catch-up to devise a browser for Windows 95. But by 1995, Gates was saying that, like the introduction of the personal computer, "the Internet is a tidal wave." Radio and then television had created what Marshall McLuhan called "The Global Village" in the course of the twentieth century. The Internet seems destined to have even more profound effects on the next century.

357.

1994—ELECTION OF NELSON MANDELA

From the twenty-sixth to the twenty-ninth of April 1994, the first nonracial election in the history of South Africa was held. Undeterred by the terrorist attacks of right-wing whites, millions of blacks voted for the leader of the African National Congress, Nelson Mandela, who was overwhelmingly elected president. The victory was a triumph not just for Mandela, but for outgoing white President F. W. de Klerk, who had negotiated with Mandela for more than two years to create a new country that put three hundred years of suppression of the black majority behind it. Nelson Mandela was sworn in as president on May 10, and on the eleventh, he named his first cabinet, which included representatives of all four of the racial groups that had been separated for so long by apartheid policies.

358.

1995—THE OKLAHOMA CITY BOMBING

A five-thousand-pound truck bomb destroyed the north side of the nine-story Alfred P. Murrah Federal Building in Oklahoma City, the state's capital, just as the workday began on April 19, 1995. The explosion killed 168 people, including 19 children in a day-care center in the building, and seriously injured another 400. A shocked country watching the rescue operations and recovery of the dead learned that the massive destruction was not the work of foreign terrorists, but of right-wing extremists, U.S. Army veterans named Timothy McVeigh and Terry Nichols. The attack was carried out on the second anniversary of the death of seventy members of a religious cult led by David Koresh at a compound near Waco, Texas, who died in a fire following a bungled federal attack on the compound after weeks of negotiations had failed. The Oklahoma bombing brought to public attention the dozens of right-wing antigovernment organizations, many of a paramilitary nature, operating in the United States. Tried separately, McVeigh and Nichols were found guilty of the bombing in 1997 and 1998, with McVeigh receiving the death penalty.

359.

1996 — CLINTON REELECTED PRESIDENT

In 1996, there was a Republican free-for-all in the early primaries, but the voters followed the usual Republican party course in the long run and gave the presidential nomination to the senior figure whose "turn" it was, Senate majority leader Robert Dole, who had been the vice-presidential candidate on the Gerald Ford ticket in 1976, and had given George Bush a tough race for the nomination in 1992. President Clinton, who had no real primary opposition, was able to start the "fall campaign" months early, and was never behind in the polls. A Democratic fund-raising scandal began to surface shortly before the election, involving illegal contributions from foreigners and the possible funneling of funds from China to the Democrats, but the Republicans had some less serious campaign finance problems of their own. Clinton's expected sixteen-point margin of victory, according to election eve polls, dwindled to eight points by the next day, but he still won easily, taking 379 electoral college votes to 159 for Dole. Ross Perot, the Texas billionaire, ran again as an independent, but his standing in the polls was not high enough to gain him entry into the presidential debates on television. His presence on the ballot, however, caused Clinton to fall just short of 50 percent of the popular vote.

360.

1997—DOLLY, A CLONED SHEEP

On February 22, 1997, the world was stunned by an announce-ment from the Roslin Institute in Edinburgh, Scotland, that an adult sheep had been cloned, producing a genetic copy named Dolly. The idea of cloning had first been proposed in 1938 by Dr. Hans Spemann of Germany, but to the public the idea had always remained something from the world of science fiction, like the clon-ing of Hitler in Ira Levin's *The Boys from Brazil*. Serious research had been pursued by a number of scientists, but a fraud perpetrated in 1983 had scared most researchers away from the field. In Scotland Dr. Ian Wilmut had quietly been working on the problem for twenty-three years. The announcement of his success with Dolly confounded scientists who had relegated cloning to the "can't be done" category, and fascinated a public that thought a creature like Dolly could exist only in a doctored photograph in a supermarket tabloid. Weighty discussion of the moral and social consequences of cloning ensued, with even the most serious thinkers suddenly confronted with the potential reality of "boys from Brazil" scenar-ios. And although Dr. Wilmut, modest to a fault, was clearly no Victor Frankenstein, it was lost on no one that nineteenth-century fantasy had once again become twentieth-century science.

361.

1997—DEATH OF PRINCESS DIANA

The death of Diana, princess of Wales, on August 31, 1997, as the result of a car crash in a Paris automobile tunnel, was the occasion for an outpouring of emotion seldom seen in the course of the century. Following her marriage to Prince Charles, heir to the British throne, in a televised ceremony at St. Paul's Cathedral in London on July 2, 1982, Princess Diana had succeeded Jacqueline Kennedy Onassis as the most renowned woman in the world. Beautiful and famous for her clothes, which were in marked contrast to the dowdiness usually associated with the British royal family, her photograph appeared on countless magazine covers around the world. As the fairy tale turned sour with the failure of her marriage to Prince Charles after the birth of their two sons, Diana gained great public sympathy through her ability to reach out to ordinary people. Her death at such a young age and in such tragic circumstances intensified the grief expressed by millions, particularly younger women who had taken her to their hearts. Because the car in which she had been traveling had been going at high speed to escape a group of paparazzi, the activities of these photographers, who followed her everywhere and could command huge prices for a single intimate photo, came under intense scrutiny. In Great Britain itself, there was an anger toward the queen that seemed to threaten the future of the throne. However, in the year that followed, Prince Charles's attention to their sons and his general demeanor had repaired much of the damage.

362.

1998—HONG KONG REVERTS TO CHINA

The British Crown Colony, an island and adjacent territory on the Chinese mainland, was acquired by Great Britain starting in 1842, and ending in 1898 with the signing of a ninety-nine-year lease of the mainland areas. A major Asian port and economic center with a society much influenced by British customs, it was returned to Chinese rule in its entirety in 1998 when the century-long lease expired. China promised that it would retain its capitalistic economy and many of the Western freedoms unknown in the rest of China. As China itself was in the process of becoming more capitalistic, this did not seem an impossible promise to keep but even so, many British subjects and Western businesses left Hong Kong before its reversion to Chinese control.

363.

1998—PEACE IN NORTHERN IRELAND

In the late 1960s, the "troubles" between Protestants and Catholics in Northern Ireland resurfaced. IRA militants from the Catholic minority began once again using terrorist techniques against the Protestant majority and its British protectors. Three decades of reciprocal bloodshed ensued in Northern Ireland, with terrorist attacks also taking place in England. In 1984, during the Conservative party conference in Brighton, an IRA bomb exploded at the Grand Hotel, killing five and injuring thirty-two, with Prime Minister Margaret Thatcher barely escaping. In the 1990s, the Clinton administration began new efforts to intervene in the Irish situation. These were welcomed by British Prime Minister John Major, but he objected to the IRA political leader Gerry Adams being given a visa to visit the United States. Clinton went ahead with issuing the visa because many experts felt that Adams must be allowed to be seen as a statesman instead of a criminal. From that point in 1994 on, progress was gradually made. President Clinton sent a personal envoy, former Senate majority leader George Mitchell, to Northern Ireland, where he spent nearly two years working with all sides to achieve an agreement that would lead to peace. The new Labour prime minister of Great Britain, Tony Blair, was also sympathetic to the American efforts, and in the spring of 1998, an agreement was signed by all parties that led to a referendum. With the passage of the referendum by both Catholic and Protestant majorities, the transition to a new political arrangement in Northern Ireland began, holding out some hope that a century-long conflict might be approaching an end.

364.

1999—IMPEACHMENT OF PRESIDENT CLINTON

Twenty-three months after being sworn in to his second term as president of the United States, William Jefferson Clinton was impeached by the House of Representatives on charges of perjury and obstruction of justice, creating the constitutional necessity of a Senate trial on whether or not to remove him from office. The charges stemmed from what the president himself admitted in August 1998 to be an "improper relationship" with a White House intern named Monica Lewinsky.

The House Judiciary Committee forwarded four articles of impeachment to the full House, and on December 19, 1998, two of the articles were passed. The first article accused Clinton of perjury for misleading the federal grand jury about the nature of his relationship with Monica Lewinsky. The second article charged Clinton with obstruction of justice for allegedly trying to cover up his relationship with Lewinsky.

The trial to convict the president began in January 1999, with the Chief Justice of the Supreme Court of the United States presiding and all one hundred senators acting as the "jury." A successful conviction would have resulted in Clinton's being the first president removed from office in an impeachment trial. President Andrew Johnson, the only other president to undergo such a trial, in 1868, survived impeachment by one vote. With public opinion polls continuing to show that nearly two thirds of the country did not want Clinton removed from office, the Senate was unable to muster a majority vote for conviction on either of the two impeachment charges. On February 12, 1999, the charge of perjury was rejected by a vote of 55 to 45. The vote on the obstruction of justice charge was split 50 to 50, but this was far from the two-thirds majority of 67 votes needed for conviction. President Clinton thus remained securely in office.

365.

1999 — THE MILLENNIUM BUG

Computers have changed the world in the second half of the twentieth century. Technology always offers the promise of perfection, but it never fully delivers. Throughout the century, technology has created problems as well as solved them. Millions of defective automobiles have been recalled, often after people were killed because of a technical problem. Planes crash, spacecraft blow up, and small household appliances go on the fritz with depressing regularity. But that is nothing compared with computers, which until very recently had a major flaw built into them. The available space for code in earlier computers was limited, and to save room, both chips and software were coded to mark the years using only two digits. What that means is that on January 1, 2000, computers all over the world could roll everything back to the year 1900. No one is entirely certain what that would mean, but there is a good chance that international financial networks could be completely disabled, and that widespread blackouts, subway breakdowns, and air traffic–control nightmares could occur. To fix the problem requires the revision of not just software code, but adjustment or replacement of billions of tiny chips. While the federal government, and the governments of other major nations, are spending billions on the millennium bug problem, there are many smaller countries, and countless businesses around the world, that have so far made little effort to deal with it. Because so many computers interact, a problem half a world away could affect major systems that have dealt with their own problems. It remains to be seen whether countering the effects of the millennium bug will be the last great success of the twentieth century or the first major problem of the twenty-first century.

I N D E X

Aaron, Henry, 99
Abie's Irish Rose, 79–80
Academy Awards, 101–102
Acheson, Lila, 79
acquired immune deficiency syndrome
    (AIDS), 241–242
Adams, Gerry, 266
Adler, Robert, 191
African National Congress, 250, 260
Afrikaner Nationalist Party, 170
Agnew, Spiro, resignation of, 224
Alamein, El, Battle of, 147
Alaska, 193
Alcock, John, 68–69
Alcoholics Anonymous (AA), 121
Aldrin, Edwin E., Jr., 217
Algeria, 36
Allen, Paul, 226–227
American Express, 176
American Federation of Labor, 125
American Revolution, 29
America's Cup, 244
Amundsen, Roald, 36
Anders, William A., 216
Anderson, Carl D., 101
Anderson, John B., 239
Anderson, Marion, 140–141
Andreessen, Marc, 259
Antiapartheid Act (1986), 249–250
anti-Semitism, 46, 76
antismoking campaign, 185
apartheid, 170
Apollinaire, Guillaume, 60
Apollo missions, 216, 217
Arlington National Cemetery, 77
Armies of the Night, The, 211
arms agreement, U.S.-Soviet (1972),
    220

Armstrong, Neil A., 217
Art Nouveau, 6
assembly line, invention of, 8
Associated Press, 160
AT&T, breakup of, 246
Atlee, Clement, 160–161
atomic bombs, 159
Audubon, John James, 24
Audubon Society, 24–25
Austro-Hungarian Empire, 49

B-29S Superfortress, 152–153
Babe Ruth, home-run record of, 98–99
baby boom, 162
Baden-Powell, Sir Robert, 32
Badoglio, Pietro, 153
Baker, Newton D., 59
Baldwin, Stanley, 124
ballot initiatives, 9
Bannister, Roger, 184
Bardeen, John, 164
Barnard, Christiaan, 214
Barrie, J. M., 21
bathyscape, 114
Batista, Fulgencio, 193
Baum, L. Frank, 5
Bayliss, Lillian, 49
Bayliss, William, 10
BBC, 99
Beatles, 206
Becky Sharp, 61
Becquerel, Antoine, 32
Begin, Menachem, 234
Belarus, 257
Belasco, David, 21
Bell, Alexander Graham, 53
Benchley, Robert, 79
Ben-Gurion, David, 169

Bennett, Floyd, 104
Berlin Wall, 201, 253
Berners-Lee, Tim, 259
Berry, Albert, 40
Bible Belt, 89
Billy Budd, 87–88
Bina, Eric, 259
Birdseye, Clarence, 57
birth control, first clinic for, 54
Black, Hugo, 146
"Black Death," 70
"Black Friday," 103–104
black holes, 133
blackout (1965), 209–210
blacks, integration of, 34, 189, 212, 213
Blair, Tony, 266
blood bank, 139
B'nai B'rith Anti-Defamation League, 46
Bohr, Niels, 101
Book-of-the-Month Club, 94
Borglum, John Gutzon, 141
Borglum, Lincoln, 142
Borman, Frank, 210, 216
Boston Red Sox, 14
Boy Scouts, 32
Brandeis, Louis, 57
Brandenburg Gate, closing of, 201
brassiere, elastic, 50–51
Brattain, Walter H., 164
Braun, Eva, 159
Braun, H.F.W., 23
Braun, Wernher von, 95
Breton, André, 61
Bretton Woods Conference, 155
Brezhnev, Leonid I., 220
Britain, Battle of, 136–137
British Commonwealth, 48, 111
Britten, Benjamin, 88
Bronze Age, 5
Brooke, Rupert, 37
Brooklyn Dodgers, 165–166
"Brother, Can You Spare a Dime?," 112–113
Brotherhood of Sleeping Car Porters, 125–126

Brown, Arthur Whitten, 68–69
Brownie cameras, 4
Brown v. Board of Education, 212, 213
Bryan, William Jennings, 3, 30, 89
bubonic plague, 70–71
Bull Moose Party, 42
Burn, Harry, 72
Bush, George, 219, 251, 256, 257
Button, Dick, 179
Byrd, Richard E., 104

cables, communications, 14
Calder, Alexander, 113
California, University of, 165, 218
California Institute of Technology, 35, 101
campaign contributions, corporate, 29
Camp David Accords, 234
cancer, cigarettes linked to, 185
Capek, Karel, 71
Capone, Al, 68, 103
car insurance, mandatory, 97
Carlson, Chester, 129
Carnarvon, earl of, 81
Carnegie, Andrew, 34
Carothers, Wallace, 133
Carson, Rachel, 202–203
Carter, Howard, 81
Carter, Jimmy, 201, 229, 230, 234, 236–237, 239
Carter, Lillian, 201
Caruso, Enrico, 9, 27
Castro, Fidel, 193–194
Castro, Raul, 193
censorship, 6
census, U.S. (1920), 75
Centers for Disease Control, U.S., 241
Chain, Ernst, 142
chain reaction, 114–115
Challenger, explosion of, 240
Chamberlain, Neville, 130
Chambers, Whittaker, 177
Chamonix, France, 84
Chanel No. 5, 78
Chaplin, Charlie, 44

Charles, Prince of Wales, 264
Charleston, the, 82–83
Chekhov, Anton, 11
Chiang Kai-shek, 117
Chicago Tribune, 171
Childhood's End, 209
China, People's Republic of, 173, 207, 212, 219, 265
chlorofluorocarbons (CFCs), 218
Christie, Agatha, 71–72
Chrysler Corporation, 148
Churchill, Winston, 131, 136, 144, 151, 153, 156, 158, 160, 162
Civil Rights Act (1957), 192
Civil War, U.S., 46, 51, 76, 211
Clarke, Arthur C., 209
Clark University, Freud at, 31
Clay, Henry, 56
Cleveland, Grover, 42, 72
Cleveland, Ohio, 37
Clinton, Hillary Rodham, 258
Clinton, William Jefferson (Bill), 171, 258, 262, 267
Coca-Cola, 26
Cold War, 184, 257
Collins, Michael, 47, 217
Columbia Broadcasting System, 171
Columbia School of Journalism, 62
Columbia (space shuttle), 240
comedy, slapstick, 44–45
comic strip, daily, 29
Common Sense Book of Baby and Child Care, 162
communism, 129–130, 188
Communist party, Soviet, 60
compact disks (CDs), 172
Company, 223
Compton, Arthur H., 148
computers, 268
Comstock, Daniel F., 61
Conant, James B., 149
Congress, U.S., 75, 109, 186–187, 192, 193, 199, 201, 221, 224, 226, 249–250
Connolly, Maureen (Little Mo), 251

conservation, 24–25, 28, 202–203
Constitution, U.S., amendments to:
  Eighth, 220–221
  Sixteenth, 46
  Eighteenth, 67–68
  Nineteenth, 74, 221
  Twenty-first, 68
  Twenty-fifth, 224, 229
  Twenty-seventh, 221
Consumer Price Index, 41–42
continental drift, 41
Coolidge, Calvin, 70, 86, 87
country music, 92
Court, Margaret, 251
Cox, Archibald, 225
Cox, James M., 74
credit cards, 176
Crick, Francis, 181
Crippen, Robert L., 240
Cuban missle crisis, 207
Cultural Revolution, in China, 212
Curie, Marie, 32, 120
Curie, Pierre, 32, 120
Czechoslovakia, Germany's annexation of, 130–131

Dalí, Salvador, 61
Dallas, TX, 205, 208
Darrow, Clarence, 89–90
Darvall, Denise, 214
Darwin, Charles, 89–90
Davidson brothers, 15
Davis, John W., 86
Dawson, Charles, 42
Dayan, Moshe, 213
daylight saving time, 65
D-day, 154
DDT, 202–203
Dean, Christopher, 245
Dean, John, 225
death penalty, 220–221
debates, presidential, first televised, 196–197
Defense Department, U.S., 151
De Forest, Lee, 82

de Gaulle, Charles, 156, 194
de Klerk, F. W., 250, 260
desegregation, 213
Detroit, MI, 187
Deukmejian, George, 187
de Valera, Eamon, 48
Dewey, Thomas E., 157, 171
Diamond v. *Chakabarty*, 238
Diana, Princess of Wales, 263–264
Dies, Martin, 129
Dillinger, John, 84
Diner's Club, 176
Dirac, Paul A. M., 101
disarmament, 199, 220
disc jockey, first, 99
Discovery (space shuttle), 254
Disney, Walt, 100
DNA (deoxyribonucleic acid), 77, 181
Doenitz, Karl, 159
Dole, Robert, 171, 262
Dolly, cloned sheep, 263
Domingo, Plácido, 9
draft, 58–59, 211, 230
Drew, Richard Charles, 139
Duchamp, Marcel, 62
Dukakis, Michael, 251–252
Dunkirk, retreat from, 136
DuPont, 131, 133
Dust Bowl, 118

Earhart, Amelia, 127–128
earthquake:
  in Japan (1923), 81–82
  in San Francisco (1906), 26–27
Easter Rebellion (1916), 47
Eastman Kodak Company, 4
East Pittsburgh, PA, 70
Eckert, J. Presper, 163–164
Ederle, Gertrude, 93–94
Edison, Thomas, 19, 82
Edward VIII, King of England, 124–125
Egypt, 213
Egypt–Israel peace treaty, 234
Ehrlichman, John D., 226

eight-hour day, 93
Einstein, Albert, 35, 55, 101
Eisenhower, Dwight D., 154, 165, 177, 178, 179–180, 188, 190, 198, 199
elections, first primary, 13–14
elections, U.S.:
  of 1904, 20
  of 1908, 30
  of 1912, 42
  of 1916, 55–56
  of 1920, 74
  of 1924, 86
  of 1928, 100
  of 1932, 112
  of 1936, 125
  of 1940, 137
  of 1944, 156
  of 1948, 171
  of 1952, 179
  of 1956, 190–191
  of 1960, 197
  of 1964, 208–209
  of 1968, 216
  of 1972, 222
  of 1976, 229
  of 1980, 239
  of 1984, 246–247
  of 1988, 251–252
  of 1992, 258
  of 1996, 262
Elgar, Edward William, 8
Eliot, T. S., 80
Elizabeth, Queen Mother of England, 125
Elizabeth II, Queen of England, 182
Ellsworth, Lincoln, 36
Empire State Building, 110–111
ENIAC, 163
Eniwetok Atoll, 180
Episcopal priests, women as, 228–229
equal rights amendment, 221
Ervin, Sam, 225
Ethiopia, famine in, 248
European Recovery Program, 165
Evans, Arthur, 5

Everest, Mount, 182
evolution, 89–90

Fair Labor Standards Act (1938), 44
Federal Bureau of Investigation, 84–85
Federal Reserve Board, 42
Feminine Mystique, The, 204
Ferdinand, Franz, Archduke,
    assassination of, 49–50
Fermi, Enrico, 115, 148
Ferraro, Geraldine, 246–247
figure skating, 179, 245
Fisher, Bud, 29
Fisher, Irving, 103
Flammarion, Camille, 33
Fleming, Alexander, 142
flight, first nonstop transatlantic, 68–69
Florey, Howard, 142
Florida's Pelican Island, 28
flu, Spanish, 64
flying machine, invention of, 13
Follies, 223
Fonteyn, Margot, 200
Food and Drug Administration, U.S.,
    202
football, 11, 26
Ford, Gerald R., 224, 229
Ford, Henry, 8, 30, 93
Forrest, Nathan Bedford, 76
fossils, dating of, 173
four-minute mile, breaking of, 184
Fox Studios, 44
France, 36, 194
Franco, Francisco, 122
Freud, Sigmund, 31, 60
Friedan, Betty, 204

Gagarin, Yuri, 200, 202
Gandhi, Mohandas K., 166, 169
Garin, Maurice, 15
Garner, John Nance, 125, 137
Gates, Bill, 226–227, 259
Gaza Strip, 213
Gemini spacecraft, 210
General Foods, 57

genetic engineering, 238
George VI, King of England, 124–125
Germany, 253
Gillette, King Camp, 18–19
Glenn, John, 202
glider, human-powered, 231–232
Goddard, Robert H., 95–96, 155
Goddard Space Center, 96, 155
Golden Age, 5
Goldmark, Peter, 171–172
gold standard, 3
Goldwater, Barry, 208, 222, 231
Golf, Grand Slam of, 106–107
Gorbachev, Mikhail, 257
Gordon, Louis "Slim," 127
Gorgas, William Crawford, 17
Göring, Hermann, 163
Gossamer Condor, 231–232
Gould, Gordon, 195
Gouney, Jay, 112
Graf, Steffi, 251
Grand Ole Opry, 92
"Great Leap Forward, The," 212
Great Train Robbery, The, 19–20
Greenwich Mean Time, 36
Gregoire, Mark, 131
Griffith, D. W., 44
Groves, Leslie R., 161
Guevara, Ernesto "Che," 193
Guggenheim Museum, 195–196
Guimard, Hector, 6

Haldeman, H. R., 226
Hale, George Ellery, 34–35
Halley's Comet, 33
Handy, W. C., 50
Harburg, E. Y., 112
Harding, Warren G., 70, 74
Harlem, 19
Harley-Davidson Motorcycles, 15–16
Harrison, George, 206
Harrison, William Henry, 216
Harvard University, 80, 167
Hawaii, 4, 193
Heath, Edward, 235

Heisenberg, Werner, 101
helicopters, 135
Herblock, 188
Hillary, Edmund, 182
Himalayas, 182
Hindenburg, Paul von, 117
Hindenburg disaster, 127
Hindus, 166, 169
Hines, Edward, 37
Hinton, M. A., 43
Hiroshima, 159, 161
Hiss, Alger, 176–177
Hitler, Adolf, 77, 117, 123–124, 130–131, 132, 136–137, 140, 145, 147, 148, 153, 155, 159
HIV, 241–242
Hofmannsthal, Hugo von, 39
Holland, John P., 23
Hollywood, see movies
Hong Kong, 265
Hoover, Herbert, 100, 112
Hoover, J. Edgar, 84–85, 146
hormones, discovery of, 10
House of Representatives, U.S., 267
House Un-American Activities Committee, 129–130, 188
Howard, Leslie, 151
Hubble Space Telescope, 240, 254
Hughes, Charles Evans, 55–56
Humphrey, Hubert H., 216
Hungarian uprising, 190
Hurley Machine Company, 28
Hussein, Saddam, 256–257
hydrogen bomb, 180
hyper-text markup language (HTML), 259

IBM, 164
ice cream cones, 21
Ickes, Harold, 141
Illinois, University of, 259
income taxes, 45
India, 70–71, 166, 169
industrialism, 7
inflation, 42
International Monetary Fund, 155–156

Internet, 259
Iran hostage crisis, 236–237
Iraq, 256–257
Ireland, 68
Ireland, Northern, 47–48, 265–266
Irish Republican Army, 47–48
"iron curtain," 162
isolationism, 58, 67
Israel, State of, 169–170, 213
Israel–Egypt peace treaty, 234
Italy, 153, 241
Iwo Jima, 158
Izvestiya, 60

Jacob, Mary Phelps, 50–51
Japanese internment camps, 145–146
Jazz Age, 82
jazz music, 50
Jazz Singer, The, 82
jeeps, 148
Jerusalem, Old, 213
John Paul I, Pope, 233
John Paul II, Pope, 229, 233
Johnson, Andrew, 267
Johnson, Lyndon B., 192, 205, 208–209, 213, 215
Johnston, Harold, 218
Joliot-Curie, Frederick, 120
Joliot-Curie, Irene, 120
Jones, Bobby, 106–107
Jones, Brian, 114
Jordan, 213, 215
Joyce, James, 116
Justice Department, U.S., 227
Just So Stories, 10–11

Kafka, Franz, 53
Kalmus, Herbert T., 61
Kassebaum, Nancy Landon, 125
Keller, Helen, 17
Kennedy, Caroline, 205
Kennedy, Edward M., 160
Kennedy, Jacqueline Bouvier, 205
Kennedy, John F., 190, 196–198, 201
    assassination of, 205, 207

Kennedy, John F., Jr., 205
Kennedy, Joseph P., 68
Kennedy, Robert F., 215
Kennedy Space Center, 240
Kerensky, Alexander, 59
Keystone Kops, 44–45
Khomeini, Ayatollah, 236–237
Khrushchev, Nikita S., 197, 207
kidney transplants, 175
King, Martin Luther, Jr., 169, 189, 205
    assassination of, 215
Kipling, Rudyard, 10
Kirov Ballet, 200
Kitty Hawk, NC, 13
Korean War, 135, 175
Ku Klux Klan, 76
Kursk, Battle of, 152
Kuwait, 256

Land, Edwin Herbert, 167–168
Landon, Alfred, 125
lasers, 195
Lawler, Richard H., 175
League of Nations, 75
League of Women Voters, 74–75
Lebanon, 213
Lehar, Franz, 24
Lend-Lease program, 138
Lenin, Vladimir, 59
Leningrad, siege of, 140
Lennon, John, 206
Lewinsky, Monica, 267
Libby, Walter, 173
Life magazine, 122
Lincoln, Abraham, 28
Lincoln Memorial, 140–141
Lindbergh, Charles A., 69, 97
Lippmann, Walter, 145
Little Night Music, A, 223
Liu Shao-ch'i, 212
Long, J. L., 21
Long March, 117
long-playing record (LP), 171
Louis XIV, King of France, 67
Lovell, James A., Jr., 210, 216

Lowell Observatory, 106
Luce, Henry, 122
Lusitania, 58

MacArthur, Douglas, 146, 175, 178
McCarthy, Joseph R., 188
McCartney, Paul, 206
McCord, James, 225
MacCready, Paul, 231
McGovern, George, 222
McGwire, Mark, 99
machine guns, 51
McKinley, William, 3, 20, 205
McVeigh, Timothy, 261
Macy's Thanksgiving Day Parade, 11
Madama Butterfly, 21
magnetron (electronic tube), 138
Magritte, René, 61
Maiman, Theodore H., 195
Major, John, 236, 265–266
Manchuria, 159
Mandela, Nelson, 250, 260
Manhattan Project, 115
Mao Tse-tung, 117, 212
march on Washington, 204–205
Marine Corps War Memorial, 158
Maris, Roger, 98–99
Marne, Battle of the, 51–52
Mars, landing on, 228
Marshall, George C., 143, 165,
    188
Marshall, Thurgood, 213
Marshall Plan, 165
Martin, Joseph, 178
Masefield, John, 136
MasterCard, 176
Mauchly, John, 163–164
Melville, Herman, 87
Mercury spacecraft, 202
Merry Widow, The, 24
Metamorphosis, The, 53
method acting, 12
Metro-Goldwyn-Mayer, 44
Mickey Mouse, 100–101
microbes, patenting of, 238

Microsoft, 226–227, 259
microwaves, 138
Midway, Battle of, 146–147
military-industrial complex, 199
millennium bug problem, 268
Miller, Glenn, 151
Milne, A. A., 96
Mindszenty, Cardinal, 190
minimum wage, 43–44
Minoans, 5
Miranda rights, 211–212
Mir space station (Russian), 240, 249
Mitchell, George, 266
Mitchell, John N., 225, 226
mobiles, 113
Model-T, 30
Molina, Mario, 218
Mondale, Walter F., 246–247
"Monkey Trial," 89–90
monopolies, 38
Monroe, James, 125
Monroe, Marilyn, 149
Montgomery, Bernard, 147, 154
Montgomery bus boycott, 189
Montreal Protocol, 218
moon, 206–207
  orbiting of, 216
  walk on, 217
Morrison, Herbert, 127
Morse code, 40
Mosaic, 259
Mount Wilson Telescope, 34–35
movies, 44, 61–62, 135
Muller v. *Oregon,* 57
Munich, Germany, 222
Museum of Modern Art, 105
Muslims, 166, 169
Mussolini, Benito, 123, 153
"Mutt and Jeff," 29

Nagasaki, 159
Nagy, Imre, 190
Naismith, James, 174

National American Woman Suffrage Association, 74
National Association for the Advancement of Colored People (NAACP), 141
National Basketball Association (NBA), 174
National Cancer Institute, 185
National Congress Party, 166
Nationalist Republic of China (Taiwan), 173, 219
National Labor Relations Act (Wagner Act) (1935), 119, 126
National Organization for Women, 204
Native Americans, citizenship granted to, 86–87
Nautilus, 184
Navratilova, Martina, 251
Nehru, Jawaharlal, 166
Neumann, John von, 163
Nevada, legalized gambling in, 109–110
New Deal, 100, 112, 119–120, 125
Newfoundland, 68
Newton, Isaac, 33
New York, NY, 19, 139, 144, 196, 209–210
New Yorker, 90
New York Times, 159–160
New York World, 62
New York World's Fair (1939), 132, 133
Nicholas II, Czar of Russia, 59
Nichols, Terry, 261
Nixon, Richard M., 177, 179, 196–198, 207, 216, 220, 222, 224, 225
Nobel Prize, 7–8
  for Chemistry, 120
  for Literature, 80, 91, 162
  for Peace, 75, 165, 215, 234, 250, 255, 257
  for Physics, 101, 148
  for Physiology or Medicine, 142, 181
Nobile, Alberto, 36
Noonan, Frederick J., 127

Northwest Passage, 36
Notre Dame, 65–66
novocaine, 23
Nuremberg war crimes tribunal, 163
Nureyev, Rudolf, 200
nylon stockings, 133–134

O'Connor, Sandra Day, 242
Oklahoma City bombing, 261
Olds, Ransome E., 8
Old Victoria Theater (Old Vic), 49
Olympic Games, 85, 179, 1924, 1952
  basketball first played in, 174
  in Berlin (1936), 123–124
  first winter, 84
  Moscow, boycott of, 239
  terrorism at (1972), 221–222
Operation Desert Storm, 256–257
Oppenheimer, J. Robert, 133, 161
orbit of earth, first U.S., 202
Oregon, 9
organ transplant, 175
Oswald, Lee Harvey, 207–208
Owens, Jesse, 124
Oxford University, 142
ozone layer, warnings about, 218

Pac-Man (video game), 243
pageant, Miss America, 73
Panama Canal, 17
Panama Canal Treaty, 230–231
Pan American Airlines, closing of,
  256
parachutes, 40
Paramount Pictures, 44
Paris, 6, 15, 47, 156
Parker, Alton B., 20
Parks, Rosa, 189
Patton, George S., 154
Peace Corps, 201
Pearl Harbor, 103, 143
penicillin, 142
Pentagon, 151–152
perestroika, 257

Perot, Ross, 258, 262
Peter Pan, 21–22
Philippines, 146
phone service, transcontinental, 53
photocopy machine (xerox), 129
Picasso, Pablo, 3, 60
Piccard, Auguste, 113–114
Piccard, Bertrand, 114
Piccard, Jacques, 114
Piltdown Man, 42–43
Pioneer 10 spacecraft, 244
Pittsburgh Pirates, 14
Planck, Max, 101
Plunkett, Roy, 131
Pluto, discovery of, 106
Poems, 37
Poirot, Hercule, 71–72
Poland, Hitler's invasion of, 132
Polaroid cameras, 167–168
polio, vaccine for, 185
"Pomp and Circumstance," 8
population control, 107
Potsdam Conference (1945), 160–161
Prague, Czechoslovakia, 53
Pravda, 60
Proclamation Day, 58–59
Prohibition, 67–68, 103
Puccini, Giacomo, 21
Puerto Rico, 4
Pulitzer prizes, 62–63

Quayle, Dan, 251

racial integration, 34, 189, 212,
  213
radio, commercial, 70
radiocarbon dating, 173
radium, isolation of, 32
Ranger 7, 206
Rankin, Jeannette, 54–55
Ray, James Earl, 215
razor blades, safety, 18–19
Reader's Digest, 79
"ready-mades," 62

Reagan, Ronald, 66, 187, 229, 236–237, 239, 242, 246–247
referendums, 9
Rehnquist, William, 242
relativity theory, 55
remote control, television, 191
reparation payments to Allied countries, 76–77
Rice, Grantland, 65
Rickey, Branch, 165
Riefenstahl, Leni, 123–124
Rite of Spring, The, 47
Robinson, Jackie, 165–166
"robot," 71
Rockefeller, John D., 38
Rockefeller, Mrs. John D., 105
rocket, liquid fuel, 95–96
Rockne, Knute, 65–66
Roe v. *Wade*, 242
Roman Catholic Church, 241
Rommel, Erwin, 147, 154
Roosevelt, Edith, 20
Roosevelt, Eleanor, 141
Roosevelt, Franklin Delano, 103, 104, 112, 115–116, 119, 125, 132, 137, 138, 141, 143, 144, 145, 151, 156–157, 158, 165, 171
Roosevelt, Theodore, 14, 18, 20, 24, 28, 42, 75, 112
Rose Bowl, 11
Rosenkavalier, Der, 38–39
"Rosie the Riveter," 149–150
Ross, Harold, 90
Rowland, F. Sherwood, 218
Royal Ballet of Great Britain, 200
R.U.R., 71
Rushmore, Mount, 141
Russia, 257
 see also Soviet Union
Russian Revolution, 59–60
Russo-Japanese War, 75

Sabin, Albert Bruce, 185
Sacco, Nicola, 98

Sacco-Vanzetti case, 98
Sadat, Anwar, 234
"St. Louis Blues," 50
St. Louis Exposition, 20–21
St. Valentine's Day massacre, 103
Salk, Jonas Edward, 185
San Francisco, CA, 26–27, 53
San Francisco Chronicle, 29
Sanger, Margaret Higgins, 54
Sarajevo, Yugoslavia, 49
Sargent, Aaron A., 72
satellites, communications, 209
Schirra, Walter M., 210
Schlafly, Phyllis, 221
Schrödinger, Erwin, 101
Scopes, John T., 89–90
Scotch tape, 89
Senate, U.S., 225, 231, 242, 267
Sennett, Mack, 44
Sergeant Pepper's Lonely Hearts Club Band, 206
Shakespeare, William, 49
Shaw, George Bernard, 91
Shepard, Alan B., Jr., 202
Sherman Antitrust Act (1890), 38
Shockley, William, 164
shopping mall, Northland, 187
Sikorsky, Igor, 135
Silent Spring, 202
Simpson, Wallis Warfield, 124–125
Sinai Peninsula, 213
Sinn Fein party, 47–48
Sirhan, Sirhan B., 215
Sirica, John J., 225, 226
Six-Day War, 213
Smith, Alfred E., 100
Social Security, 41, 42, 119–120
solar power, 186
Solidarity, 255
Somme, Battle of the, 56
Sondheim, Stephen, 223
sonic boom, 167
Sony v. *Universal Studios*, 245
Sosa, Sammy, 99

SOS distress code, 40
South Africa, 170, 249–250
South Dakota, 141
South Korea, invaded by North Korea, 175
South Pole, reaching of, 36
Soviet Union, 60, 123, 140, 159, 177, 180, 199–200, 217, 239, 257
space, first rendezvous in, 210
space shuttle, 240
Spanish-American War, 4
Spanish Civil War, 122
Spanish flu epidemic, 64
Spemann, Hans, 263
sperm, frozen, 183
Spirit of St. Louis, 97
Spock, Benjamin, 162
Stafford, Thomas P., 210
Stalin, Joseph, 59–60, 140, 158–159, 160
Standard Oil, breakup of, 38
Stanislavsky, Constantin, 12
Starling, Ernest, 10
Starr, Ringo, 206
"Star-Spangled Banner," 109
"Steamboat Willie," 100–101
Stevenson, Adlai E., III, 179–180, 190–191
Stimson, Henry L., 138
stock market crash (1929), 103–104
Stone, Christopher, 99
Strauss, Richard, 38–39
Stravinsky, Igor, 47
Stultz, Wilbur, 127
submarine, nuclear-powered, 184
submarines, U.S. Army, 23
subway, 19
suffrage movement, 72–73
Sullivan, Annie, 17
Sullivan, Thomas, 18
Supreme Court, U.S., 56, 57, 68, 189, 211–212, 213, 220–221, 225, 238, 242, 245
surgery, on the unborn, 254

Suribachi, Mount, 158
"surrealist," 60–61
Syria, 213
Szilard, Leo, 114–115, 148

Taft, William H., 30, 42
Taiwan, 173, 219
tanks, 56, 152
taxes, income, 45
tea bags, 18
technicolor movies, 61–62
Teflon (polytetrafluorethylene), 131
Tennis, Grand Slam of, 251
territories, U.S., 4
terrorism, 221–222, 236–237, 260, 261
Thatcher, Margaret, 235–236, 265
Thomas, Clarence, 213
3M Company, 89
Three-Mile Island nuclear accident, 235
Three Sisters, The, 11–12
Thurmond, J. Strom, 192
Titanic, 40
Tombaugh, Clyde W., 106
Torvill, Jayne, 245
Toscanini, Arturo, 140
Tour de France, 15
traffic lights, first, 37
transatlantic flight, first commercial, 134
transistors, 164
transplant, heart, 214
Trotsky, Leon, 59–60
Truman, Harry, 157, 160, 161, 165, 171, 175
Tucker, Ruth, 175
Tut-Ankh-Amen, King (King Tut), 81
2001: A Space Odyssey, 209

Ukraine, 257
ultraviolet rays, 218
Ulysses, 116
unemployment compensation, 120
unions, 93, 125–126, 255
United Automobile Workers, 93
United Nations, 144, 155, 178, 190, 219

United Nations Security Council, 175

Universal Studios, 44

UNIX code, 259

Unknown Soldier, Tomb of the, 77

V-1 rockets, 155

Valentino, Rudolph, 94–95

Van Buren, Martin, 251

Vanzetti, Bartolelmeo, 98

Vatican, 241

Versailles, Treaty of, 67

Vickers Vimy bomber, 68

Victoria, Queen of England, 166
   death of, 7

video taping, legalization of, 245

Vietnam War, 135, 211, 222, 230

Viking 1 (spacecraft), 228

Visa, 176

Volstead Act (1919), 67–68

Vostok (sputnik), 200

Wagner, Robert F., 119

Wagner Act (1935), 119, 126

Walesa, Lech, as president of Poland, 255

Walkman, Sony (tape player), 238

Wallace, DeWitt, 79

Wallace, George C., 216

Wallace, Henry A., 137, 157

Walsh, Don, 114

Warner Brothers, 44

Warren, Earl, 146, 208, 211–212

Warren Commission report, 207–208

washing machines, electric, 28

Washington, D.C., march on, 204–205

Washington, George, 23

Washkansky, Louis, 214

"Waste Land, The," 80

Watergate conspirators, 226

Watson, James Dewey, 181

Watson, Thomas A., 53

Watson, Thomas J., 164

Wayne, John, 230–231

Wegener, Alfred, 41

Weissmuller, Johnny, 85

Welch, Joseph, 188

Westminster Abbey, 182

Wheeler, John Archibald, 133

White, Walter, 141

Williams, Bert, 34

Willkie, Wendell L., 137

Wilmut, Ian, 263

Wilson, Woodrow, 42, 55–56, 57, 58, 67, 68, 72, 75, 109

Winnie the Pooh, 96

Wizard of Oz, The, 5

women's liberation movement, 204

Wonderful Wizard of Oz, The, 5–6

World Bank, 155–156

World Cup, 107–108

World Series, 14–15

World's Fair, 20

World War I, 50, 51–52, 56, 59, 61, 64, 65, 67, 68, 69, 73, 76, 77
   U.S. entry into, 58

World War II, 4, 28, 40, 67, 95, 117, 123, 132, 135
   end of, in Europe, 159–160
   U.S. entry into, 143

World Wide Web, 259

Wright, Frank Lloyd, 195–196

Wright, Orville, 13

Wright, Wilbur, 13

Yalta Conference (1945), 158–159

Yamamoto, Isoroku, 146

Yeager, Charles "Chuck," 167

yellow fever, 17–18

Yellowstone National Park, 28

Yeltsin, Boris, 257

YMCA, 174

Young, John W., 240

Ziegfeld, Flo, 83

Ziegfeld Follies, 34, 82